About the Cover

This photo montage, created specifically for this book, shares the history and spirit of nursing at Mayo Clinic.

1. Edith Graham, R.N., with the nursing diploma she received in 1889 from Women's Hospital of Chicago.
2. Saint Marys Hospital, the first hospital in Rochester, Minnesota, opened in 1889.
3. A nurse and Charles H. Mayo, M.D., examined an infant, circa 1930s.
4. The first graduates of Saint Marys Training School, classes of 1908 and 1909.
5. Saint Marys Training School nurses observed a surgical procedure, circa 1913.
6. From right: Alice Magaw, R.N., nurse anesthetist, Sister Joseph Dempsey, surgical assistant to William J. Mayo, M.D. (with back turned), collaborated during an operation, circa 1904.
7. The Croix de Guerre (French War Cross) awarded to Florence Bullard, R.N., for bravery during World War I.
8. A Saint Marys Hospital nurse holds surgical instruments used in a procedure, circa 1919.
9. Teruko Yamashita Okimoto, R.N., a cadet nurse and graduate of Saint Marys School of Nursing, circa 1945.
10. Charles Henry, L.P.N., class of 1952, the first male student at the Rochester School of Practical Nursing and Homemaking.
11. Methodist-Kahler School of Nursing students studied anatomy, circa 1950s.
12. Hand holding—an international symbol of care and comfort—represents the spirit of nursing at Mayo Clinic.
13. Saint Marys Training School nurses studied in the library, circa 1924.
14. Myrisia Fernandez, R.N., an infusion therapy nurse at Mayo Clinic in Rochester, Minnesota, involved in patient care.
15. Rhonda Sullivan, R.N., a wound, ostomy, and continence nurse at Mayo Clinic in Florida.
16. Mellissa Barth, R.N., Mayo Clinic in Rochester, Minnesota, educates nurses about the heart.
17. Joseph Carlson, R.N., a nurse anesthetist at Mayo Clinic in Rochester, Minnesota.
18. *Forever Caring,* a bronze tableau in Rochester, Minnesota, honors the history and evolution of nursing at Mayo Clinic.
19. From left : Linda Schneider, R.N., Thomas Carmody, M.D., Robert Wiechmann, M.D., Kirk Herzog P.A., and Michelle Hillesheim, R.N., worked together to repair a patient's heart valve at Mayo Clinic Health System in Eau Claire, Wisconsin.
20. Kristi Harris, R.N., Mayo Clinic in Arizona, in the ICU .
21. Habibo Haji, R.N., Mayo Clinic in Rochester, Minnesota, provided nursing care over the telephone.
22. Erin Deering, R.N., Mayo Clinic in Rochester, Minnesota, assisted a patient.
23. Susan Sanderson, L.P.N., discussed patient care with a provider at Mayo Clinic Health System in Albert Lea, Minnesota.

The
Nurses of Mayo Clinic

Caring Healers

Arlene Keeling, Ph.D., R.N., F.A.A.N.

ISBN-10: 1-893005-83-6
ISBN-13: 978-1-893005-83-9

The triple-shield Mayo Clinic logo and the words MAYO and MAYO CLINIC are marks of Mayo Foundation for Medical Education and Research.

Please address inquiries to:
Adam Holland, R.N.
Department of Nursing Administration
Mayo Clinic
200 First Street SW
Rochester, MN USA
55905
(507) 255-4551
holland.adam@mayo.edu

Printed by *Walsworth Print Group*

This book is published in association

with the Mayo Clinic Sesquicentennial

2014

"Mayo Clinic is a special place because of the people who work here and the patients we serve. We thank each and every one of you for your dedication to patient care, for being the people you are, and for your involvement in the current and future success of our organization. Everything around us will change, but two things will never change at Mayo Clinic—our commitment to our patients and our commitment to our staff."

Excerpt from a message to staff in 2010 by
Doreen Frusti, R.N., and Pamela Johnson, R.N.

Dedication

This book is respectfully dedicated to

the nurses of Mayo Clinic—past, present, and future—

whose commitment to excellence upholds the primary value of Mayo Clinic:

The Needs of the Patient Come First.

MAYO CLINIC EXPRESSES APPRECIATION

TO THE FOLLOWING BENEFACTORS FOR THEIR GENEROUS SUPPORT

OF THE PUBLICATION OF THIS BOOK

Saint Marys Hospital Auxiliary Volunteers

John T. Blozis through the Anna Blozis Fund for Nursing at Saint Marys Hospital

Rochester Methodist Hospital Auxiliary Volunteers, in recognition

of their 60th anniversary in 2014 of partnering with nurses to meet the needs of patients

Methodist-Kahler School of Nursing Alumni Association

"Because I'm continually inspired by you, our staff, and your unwavering commitment to put the needs of our patients first and do what is necessary for this organization to succeed—thank you for all you do for our patients and the support that you provide to each other during these challenging times."

—*Pamela Johnson, R.N.*

Staff

AUTHOR
Arlene Keeling, Ph.D., R.N., F.A.A.N.

EXECUTIVE COMMITTEE
Pamela Johnson, R.N., Chair

Karen Barrie

Matthew Dacy

Adam Holland, R.N.

Kristine Johnson, R.N.

Renee Ziemer

Amy Zwygart, R.N.

PROJECT MANAGERS AND EXECUTIVE EDITORS
Matthew Dacy

Adam Holland, R.N.

ART DIRECTOR
Karen Barrie

PHOTOGRAPHER
Joseph Kane

COVER ART DESIGN
Steve Orwoll

ADMINISTRATIVE ASSISTANT
Renae Shellum

The Doctors Mayo: William Worrall, M.D. (center), with his sons, Charles Horace (left) and William James (right), created a unique model of care, which today makes Mayo Clinic a globally recognized center of hope and healing. Throughout the history of the Mayo practice, nurses have been key members of the team, advancing the mission of service to patients.

Table of Contents

The Nurses of Mayo Clinic: Caring Healers describes the integral role of Mayo Clinic nurses in contributing to the unparalleled recognition that Mayo Clinic has achieved around the world. We are indebted and deeply grateful to all Mayo nurses, whose care throughout generations is the inspiration for this book.

Nurses at Mayo Clinic meet their patients' needs with understanding and compassion— and the highest standards of professionalism. Our nurses make a difference through their commitment to excellence as well as by demonstrating the individual and collective impact they have on the patient care experience and the changing health care environment.

While always keeping the needs of the patient first, Mayo nurses have encouraged, listened, comforted, and cared for their patients and, most importantly, "touched" patients with their presence. Their stories are stimulating, motivating, inspiring, and at times, courageous. We hope you enjoy them.

John H. Noseworthy, M.D.
President and CEO
Mayo Clinic

Pamela O. Johnson, R.N.
Chief Nursing Officer
Mayo Clinic

Edith Graham

December 25, 1887

A Note About Names

As one might expect with an organization whose roots go back to the nineteenth century, there is a wide variety of usage for institutional and individual names in the historical record. In creating this book, we seek a balance of accuracy, using nomenclature that is appropriate for the period of time being described, along with clarity, for the general reader who wants to appreciate the story without getting lost in minutia. Here is an overview of some of the most common naming issues:

The Doctors Mayo

This book highlights three generations of physicians in the Mayo family. We include middle names when the person was known by that usage and middle initials to identify individuals who shared given names. We also include nicknames by which the physicians were familiarly known to contemporaries and by which they are referred to today: **William Worrall Mayo, M.D. (Dr. W.W. Mayo), 1819-1911**; his eldest surviving son, **William James Mayo, M.D. (Dr. Will), 1861-1939**; Dr. W.W. Mayo's youngest son, **Charles H. Mayo, M.D. (Dr. Charlie), 1865-1939**; Dr. Charlie's son, **Charles William Mayo, M.D. (Dr. Chuck), 1898-1968.**

The Sisters of Saint Francis

Since most Sisters before the Second Vatican Council were given the consecrated name Mary (such as **Sister Mary Joseph Dempsey**), we have omitted that usage for brevity and used a shorter form such as **Sister Joseph Dempsey,** with **Sister Joseph** on subsequent reference. The exception is **Sister Mary Brigh Cassidy** for whom Mary was part of a combined first name. Also, since this book focuses on nursing, we have added **R.N.** to the names of Sisters who held this professional designation.

Consistent with Mayo Clinic style, we do not list other academic degrees beyond the terminal degrees of M.D., Ph.D., and J.D.

Mayo Clinic

Until the early 1900s, the Mayo medical practice was known by informal and evolving names such as "Mayo Brothers," "Mayo's," and "The Mayo." The organization's official title was based on the partners' names at any given time, such as "The Doctors Mayo, Stinchfield, Graham, Plummer, and Judd," an approach that became increasingly unwieldy. The name **Mayo Clinic** evolved from physicians who visited Rochester to observe the Mayo brothers in surgery and referred to these educational sessions as "The Mayos' Clinic." Railroad promotions, patients, and the popular press adapted this title to "Mayo Clinic." The name became official with the opening of the first Mayo Clinic building in 1914.

Until 1986, Mayo Clinic was an outpatient practice. That year, Mayo Clinic formed a shared governance structure with Rochester Methodist Hospital and Saint Marys Hospital. Prior to that time, while the outpatient and inpatient practices collaborated closely on many levels, Mayo Clinic and both hospitals were legally separate organizations. Today, the name "Mayo Clinic" encompasses inpatient as well as outpatient care.

In 1986, Mayo Clinic opened in Jacksonville, Florida.

In 1987, Mayo Clinic opened in Scottsdale, Arizona.

Starting in 1992, a system of community-based clinics, hospitals, and other providers was developed as part of the Mayo Clinic organizational structure. Known in its early days as **Mayo Health System,** it is now called **Mayo Clinic Health System.** Sites in the Health System are located in geographic proximity to Mayo Clinic locations in Rochester, Minnesota, and Jacksonville, Florida.

In 2011, **Mayo Clinic Care Network** was established to build collaborative and information-sharing relationships with independent, community-based providers on a national and international basis.

Hospitals

In 1889, Mother Alfred Moes established **St. Mary's Hospital.**
By the middle years of the twentieth century, variations of this name
occurred such as **St. Marys Hospital, Saint Mary's Hospital,** and
Saint Marys Hospital with inconsistent use of abbreviations and
apostrophes. In this book, we make the somewhat arbitrary decision
of switching from **St. Mary's Hospital** to **Saint Marys Hospital** with
the chapter beginning in 1940, since that date closely followed the
1939 deaths of the Mayo brothers and longtime hospital superintendent Sister Joseph Dempsey. **Saint Marys** became the official name
of the hospital in 1968, when it was established as a legal entity that
was separate from the Sisters' congregation. Buildings at Saint Marys
are named in honor of Franciscan Sisters and those who were leaders
of the hospital. In 1996, a specialized pediatric inpatient facility
called **Mayo Eugenio Litta Children's Hospital** was established
within Saint Marys Hospital.

In addition, Mayo Clinic physicians and surgeons practiced
at several smaller hospitals in downtown Rochester. In 1907,
responding to patient demand and the need for accommodations
for postoperative patients as well as the family and friends who
accompanied them, business leader John Kahler developed an
innovative hotel-hospital concept. It combined surgical wards,
recovery areas, and places for guests to stay. While other individuals
and businesses managed hospitals at various times, John Kahler and
the Kahler Corporation dominated the inpatient services known
collectively as **"the downtown hospitals."** Between 1907 and 1954,
the Kahler enterprise developed or purchased hospital facilities
including the **Kahler Hotel, Zumbro Hotel, Colonial Hospital,
Worrall Hospital and Annex, Curie Hospital,** and **Olmsted Hospital.**
After World War II, the for-profit hospital model was not sustainable
for the Kahler Corporation., which left the hospital industry and
focused on hospitality-related businesses.

In 1954, **Rochester Methodist Hospital** was established as a
not-for-profit organization, providing inpatient care in downtown
Rochester. For its first twelve years, Rochester Methodist Hospital
used the former Colonial and Worrall Hospital facilities. In 1966,
Rochester Methodist Hospital opened a new building, which was
named the George M. Eisenberg Building in 1989 to honor a
longtime patient and benefactor.

Following the 1986 integration of Mayo Clinic with the two
hospitals, the names Rochester Methodist Hospital and Saint Marys
Hospital were retained under an informal collective term, "Mayo
Medical Center," which is no longer in use. Starting in the late 1990s,
Rochester Methodist Hospital and Saint Marys Hospital retained their
names under the organization's official brand name of Mayo Clinic.

In 2014, both hospitals became a single-licensed provider known
as **Mayo Clinic Hospital—Rochester.** The names **Saint Marys
Campus** and **Methodist Campus** now designate the single hospital's
two locations and acknowledge their historic roots.

In 1998, **Mayo Clinic Hospital** opened in Phoenix, expanding
Mayo's Arizona campus to two sites. Collectively, the inpatient and
outpatient practices on the Scottsdale and Phoenix campuses are
known as **Mayo Clinic in Arizona.**

In 2006, Mayo Clinic opened a hospital that physically adjoins
the outpatient practice on the Jacksonville, Florida, campus. This
hospital does not have a separate name. The combined inpatient and
outpatient services are referred to as **Mayo Clinic in Florida.**

Schools of Nursing

From 1906 to 1994, several schools in Rochester awarded the
professional designations of R.N. (registered nurse) and L.P.N.
(licensed practical nurse). The schools were affiliated with St. Mary's
Hospital and the Kahler Corporation/Rochester Methodist Hospital. As
with their sponsoring hospitals, the schools changed names several times.

R.N. Diploma

Saint Marys Training School for Nurses, established in 1906;
renamed Saint Marys Hospital School of Nursing in 1932; renamed
Saint Marys School of Nursing in 1949; closed in 1970.

L.P.N. Diploma

Rochester School of Practical Nursing and Homemakers established
in 1948; renamed Saint Marys School of Practical Nursing in 1980;
closed in 1994 .

R.N. Diploma

Colonial Hospital Training School for Nurses, established in 1918;
renamed Kahler Hospital's School of Nursing in 1921; renamed
Methodist-Kahler School of Nursing in 1954; closed in 1970.

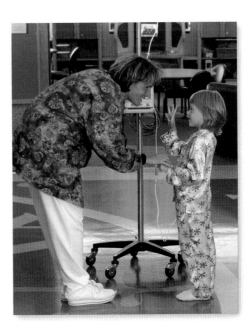

*"In the Mayo Model of Care, you are called upon to see the
patients that have the greatest health care challenges and therefore
the patients that are most frightened; and often the patients who
have come from the furthest distance; and often they come from
different cultures and different backgrounds; and you meet their
needs on a regular basis; and for that we are deeply grateful."*

— *John Noseworthy, M.D.*

Mayo Clinic Nursing Professional Practice Model

The Mayo Clinic Nursing Professional Practice Model defines nursing practice at Mayo Clinic. It is based upon relationship-based care that builds the nurse-patient relationship, resulting in appropriate, dedicated, and personalized care. It contains the nursing core values and describes the work of nurses every day through roles in care delivery. While aligning with the Mayo Clinic Model of Care, it distinguishes nursing from the medical model of care.

The foundation for the nursing model is based upon the core values of:

Evidence-based practice: Nursing care is based upon the best available evidence, including: research findings, quality improvement activities, clinical expertise, and patient values.

RN accountability: The registered nurse is accountable for the planning, implementation, evaluation, and communication of nursing care.

Professional environment: Nurses are provided authority and accountability for nursing practice and support for professional development; interdisciplinary collaboration is present.

Continuity of care: Nurses build relationships with patients and families and when care transitions occur, they are both safe and coordinated.

Nursing at Mayo is enabled through seven roles of the nurse:

Caring Healer: The nurse initiates and establishes a patient-centered relationship with an intentional therapeutic presence and culturally appropriate individualized care.

Problem Solver: The nurse utilizes critical thinking skills and innovation in daily care while offering options that are sensitive to patient wishes and personalized to individual need.

Navigator: The nurse is skilled in coordinating and prioritizing events in the patient episode of care, helping navigate through the health care system between inpatient, outpatient, and home or continuing care.

Teacher: The nurse develops and implements an educational plan for patients in all settings based on teaching theory and uses different teaching styles based on patient need.

Pivotal Communicator: The nurse communicates organized data with timeliness, clarity, and with a calm dignity to alleviate anxiety and promote understanding while linking the patient with the interdisciplinary team through collaboration.

Vigilant Guardian: The nurse plans for and provides safe patient care, anticipating vulnerabilities, using safety devices and equipment to prevent harm while collecting and assessing physiological data to intervene promptly when needed.

Transformational Leader: The nurse is a visionary, identifying and communicating ideals for the future while acting as an agent of change so they become the shared goals of all, and contributes to the collective professional voice of nursing at Mayo Clinic.

**The Mayo Nursing Professional Practice Model is
a *relationship-based care* model
Built upon the foundation of the four *Mayo Nursing Core Values*
Enabled by the *seven nursing roles***

Mayo Clinic Values

These values, which guide Mayo Clinic's mission today,
express the vision and intent of our founders, the original
Mayo physicians and the Sisters of St. Francis.

Primary Value
The needs of the patient come first.

Respect
Treat everyone in our diverse community, including patients,
their families, and colleagues, with dignity.

Compassion
Provide the best care, treating patients and family members
with sensitivity and empathy.

Integrity
Adhere to the highest standards of professionalism, ethics, and
personal responsibility, worthy of the trust our patients place in us.

Healing
Inspire hope and nurture the well-being of the whole person,
respecting physical, emotional, and spiritual needs.

Teamwork
Value the contributions of all, blending the skills of individual
staff members in unsurpassed collaboration.

Excellence
Deliver the best outcomes and highest quality service through
the dedicated effort of every team member.

Innovation
Infuse and energize the organization, enhancing the lives of those we
serve, through the creative ideas and unique talents of each employee.

Stewardship
Sustain and reinvest in our mission and extended communities by
wisely managing our human, natural, and material resources.

In this 1862 family portrait, Dr. William Worrall Mayo held daughters Phoebe (center), and Gertrude.
His wife, Louise, held William. Their youngest son, Charles, was born three years later.

NURSING ON THE FRONTIER

1851-1888

It might be said that Louise Abigail Mayo was the first "Mayo nurse"—one who epitomized "relationship-based caring" long before the phrase was coined.[1] She assumed the role without any formal training in 1851 when she married William Worrall Mayo, M.D., (Dr. W.W. Mayo) who had recently graduated from Indiana Medical College in LaPorte.

At that time, a small-town doctor often counted on his wife to help his practice. In nineteenth-century America, "almost every woman could expect to spend some part of her life caring for the infirmities and illnesses of relatives or friends."[2] For the doctor's wife, this outreach often extended to the entire community in which her husband practiced. No doubt that was the case for Louise Mayo. Her husband needed her help. From 1849, when he began his medical career by mentoring with a senior physician, until 1889, when he hired Edith Graham, R.N., as his

Louise Mayo may be considered the first nurse in the Mayo medical practice.

office nurse and anesthetist, Dr. Mayo practiced medicine as most physicians of the time did— *without* a professional nurse to assist him.[3]

A Caring Healer

Actually, Dr. Mayo needed not only his wife's help but also her expertise. In the mid nineteenth century, most people sought care from regular physicians only when they were critically ill or injured. Usually, they turned to local midwives or herbalists, or took care of themselves at home, using botanical remedies. It was in this area that Louise Mayo excelled. As a self-taught botanist, she could identify numerous plants and their therapeutic properties, and combine them according to specific recipes. For example, she would have known that quinine was a treatment for malaria; rose petals in water were used to bathe the temples for a headache; and extract of belladonna was recommended

3

to relieve gastrointestinal and bladder spasms. Given her knowledge of plants, it is likely that Louise Mayo advised her husband, or perhaps, crushed herbs with her mortar and pestle and mixed remedies for his patients.[4] Dr. Mayo used herbal medicines, sometimes in combination with other drugs like laudanum, morphine, and opium. Writing on January 2, 1867, for example, he described treating a woman with "uterine problems complicated by bladder infection" with "opii [opium] grs. ¼ and belladonna extract."[5]

Louise Mayo assisted her husband in other ways. She served as a sounding board for his ideas. As financial manager of the family, she supported his purchase of books and medical equipment.[6] One instance stands out. After a trip to New York City and other eastern medical centers, Dr. Mayo brought home a brochure describing a new microscope. Despite the fact that they would have to mortgage their house to afford the six hundred dollar instrument, his wife agreed to the purchase. She stated, "Well, William, if you could do better by the people with this new microscope and you really think you need it, we'll do it."[7]

Her help was equally important in routine matters. No doubt she packed food and coffee to sustain Dr. Mayo as he traveled by horse and buggy to make house calls. On rare occasions she accompanied him, but usually, working in log cabins out on the prairie, Dr. Mayo had to turn to a patient's family members to lend him a hand.[8] For example, on January 11, 1866, he recorded that the father and sister of a man with

"Well William, if you think you can do better by the people with this new microscope and you really think you need it, we'll do it."

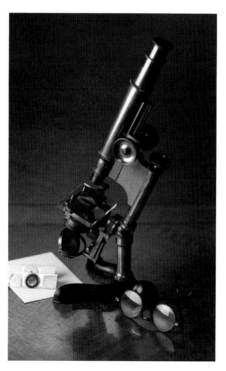

Dr. W.W. and Louise Mayo mortgaged their home to purchase a microscope so his patients could receive optimal care.

frostbite served as his assistant surgeons while he operated.[9] In Rochester, he had help from Caroline Carpenter, described as a "capable practical nurse" in whose home he performed surgery and boarded patients.[10]

Under the preceptor method that was typical for medical education, aspiring physicians or practitioners who wanted to enhance their skills might observe or participate in an operation. Working under Dr. Mayo's instructions, these assistants would pass instruments, deliver anesthesia, or help apply dressings and splints. At other times, they simply held the patient still.[11]

When Dr. Mayo was out and people arrived at the house looking for him, Louise Mayo filled in. She was well suited to the work, having "energy, determination and intelligence quite equal" to her husband.[12] As their youngest son recalled:

Patients used to call at the house for Father. There were no telephones, and if Mother knew he was out in the country, she would keep the patients interested, discussing their troubles and problems, until he returned, even if she had to prepare a meal for them. Often the neighbors and the country people came to talk to her...with as much satisfaction from a social standpoint as they got from consulting my father when sickness descended on them. When Father was taking special studies in the East or in Europe, patients came to Mother to talk about illness and she told them of the simple remedies, which would tide them through the most common illness. Mother was a real good doctor herself.[13]

Such praise notwithstanding, Louise Mayo might also have been considered an *excellent* nurse. She developed authentic caring relationships with patients; she solved problems; and she related to patients with sensitivity and compassion. Indeed, she was an integrator of care, incorporating women's cultural healing values, while providing friendship and support as part of the women's traditional healing network.[14]

That network was important. Before 1873, when the first nursing schools opened in New York, Boston, and New Haven, there were few trained nurses in the United States.[15] In general, wives, mothers, or older sisters cared for sick family members at home. Hospitals were places for the poor rather than the multiclass, acute-care facilities of today.

Babies were born at home, usually under the care of the local midwife.[16] In and around Rochester, perhaps the most skilled midwife at this time was Jane Twentyman Graham. Over the years,

Dr. W. W. Mayo often traveled to see patients, and even perform surgery, in their homes.

she delivered 243 infants without problems or death.[17] Occasionally, when she encountered complications, she may have asked Dr. Mayo for help. For example, on January 1, 1867, he wrote that he had been called to assist in a particularly long labor. According to his note, the mother had been in labor all night without progress, despite being fully dilated, and he had to break her water allowing the delivery of a healthy boy.[18] Even in these early years of medicine and nursing, professional collaboration was the key to a positive outcome.

The Path to Rochester

With skilled, compassionate providers like Dr. Mayo and his wife Louise, as well as midwife Jane Graham, Rochester had remarkable medical resources for a frontier town. It was an energetic community of newcomers and immigrants.

Like many adventure-seeking young men in the mid-nineteenth century, William Worrall Mayo had sailed from his home country of England in 1846 to make a fresh life in America. Shortly after arriving in New York City, he began a varied career, working first as a chemist at Bellevue Hospital, then journeying west and taking on a vast array of jobs ranging from a "pharmacist, tailor, physician and surgeon, census taker, farmer, newspaper publisher, justice of the peace, ferryboat operator and a veterinarian."[19]

He continued these frequent moves and career changes, graduating from Indiana Medical College in 1850, getting married in 1851, and earning a second medical degree, from what is now Washington University, in 1854. During this time, Dr. and Mrs. Mayo started a family that would eventually include six children, two of whom died in infancy.[20]

In 1864, ready to set down roots, the talented physician opened a practice in Rochester, buying space in the local newspaper to advertise his location. Dr. Mayo's reason for settling in Rochester was his

Rochester, Minnesota, was a thriving community when the Mayo family settled there during the Civil War.

appointment by President Abraham Lincoln to the military enrollment board that was located there. His job was to perform medical evaluations for men who were entering the northern army during the Civil War. The military work that originally brought Dr. Mayo to Rochester lasted barely a year, but he easily made the transition to private practice. Settling in, he purchased land in downtown Rochester (site of the Siebens Building on the Mayo Clinic campus today) and built a home for himself and Louise, along with their children, Gertrude Emily, William James, and Phoebe Louise. Their last child, Charles Horace, was born at home in 1865.[21]

Settling in Rochester was a good decision. It was a thriving farm town situated at the center of a system of river valleys in the cornfields of southeastern Minnesota. It had a population of about 3,000 and a flourishing downtown. In fact, Rochester had long been a stopover for caravans of covered wagons traveling on the Dubuque Trail from Dubuque, Iowa, to St. Paul, Minnesota. In 1864, another important link to the wider world was established when the Winona and St. Peter Railroad connected Rochester to the Mississippi River area.[22] That year, wheat yields and prices brought a new prosperity to the region.[23]

Over the next several decades, events would unfold that led to dramatic changes in his practice, and his wife would no longer be his sole source of professional help. Both sons eventually entered the medical profession and earned worldwide recognition as "Dr. Will" and "Dr. Charlie." The growth of the city with its rising opportunities for business and trade was one developmental influence. Another was an act of nature.

DR. MAYO,

OFFICE ON THIRD St.

Rochester, Minn.

OZORA P. STEARNS,

Attorney and Counselor at Law, and County Attorney for Olmsted County. Office in Graham's Block, Broadway, Rochester, Minn.

HUFF HOUSE,

HEWITT'S

ORON(

G. A. HEWITT &

Extensive Stab
dation of horses
this house,

O. P. W

County Treasurer,
Notary Public an

R OCHESTER,

This notice in the Rochester newspaper was one of the first announcements of the medical practice that Dr. W.W. Mayo established in 1864.

The Tornado of 1883

On August 21, 1883, the mayor of Rochester, Minnesota, telegraphed state Governor Lucius Hubbard:

ROCHESTER IS IN RUINS. TWENTY-FOUR PEOPLE WERE KILLED. OVER FORTY ARE SERIOUSLY INJURED. ONE-THIRD OF THE CITY LAID WASTE. WE NEED IMMEDIATE HELP.[24]

A tornado had whipped through the area late that summer day, destroying houses and scattering boards and timber, along with hail that was three to four inches in diameter.[25] Over a large area, barns and crops were entirely destroyed. Injured people and livestock were strewn throughout the countryside. More than one hundred houses were ripped from their foundations, churches and other buildings lay in ruins, and thousands of trees were stripped bare. The streets of Rochester were blocked with debris of every kind.[26] In the north end of town, hundreds of people were without shelter. Throughout Olmsted County, thirty-one people died.[27]

Many survivors suffered serious traumatic wounds that required surgery or the splinting of broken bones. Responding immediately to the crisis, Dr. Mayo took charge in Buck's Hotel, performing surgery on an old oak table.[28] In an early example of teamwork, he received help that was urgently needed. His eldest son, William James Mayo, M.D. (Dr. Will), had just joined the practice, having graduated from medical school at the University of Michigan less than two months before. Charles Horace Mayo (known as Dr. Charlie upon graduation from medical school in 1888), the younger brother, was an 18-year-old student living at home; he was already developing medical and surgical skills. In addition, the Sisters of Saint Francis, a Catholic teaching order, admitted casualties to the Academy of Our Lady of Lourdes, a short distance from downtown.

A tornado devastated Rochester in 1883 and led to a unique partnership in healing between the Doctors Mayo and the Franciscan Sisters.

Recognizing that he needed a central place to provide care, Dr. Mayo soon transferred the injured to a temporary hospital set up in a local dance hall. Also aware that he needed reliable, round-the-clock help rather than depending on volunteers who left in the evening to attend their own families, he turned to Mother Alfred Moes, founder of the community of Franciscan Sisters in Rochester. She appointed four Sisters to help him, two working by day and two by night. Despite having no medical training, the Sisters rose to the challenge, delivering care and supervising other

When the crisis was over, it became clear that nothing had been done to address the larger issue: Rochester needed a hospital.

temporary nurses until the makeshift hospital closed.[29] The immediate problem was solved. However, when the crisis was over, it became clear that nothing had been done to address the larger issue: Rochester needed a hospital.

"With our faith and hope and energy, it will succeed." [30]
To Mother Alfred, solving the problem of building a hospital was straightforward. Having founded and led several congregations, and whose work included establishing schools throughout the Midwest, she knew that Catholic Sisters were building hospitals in other parts of the United States.

As recently as 1882, the Sisters of the Holy Cross had opened St. Joseph's Hospital in South Bend, Indiana, and the Sisters of Mercy had opened a twenty-bed hospital in Minneapolis, Minnesota.[31] On December 31, 1883, barely four months after the tornado, the Franciscan Sisters of Perpetual Adoration would open a hospital (which later became part of the Mayo Clinic Health System) in La Crosse, Wisconsin, not far from Rochester.[32]

Mother Alfred knew that she had the talent, vision, and skills to establish a hospital. She also had Sisters of her congregation to take care of the patients. One problem remained: The hospital would need physicians.

Newspaper reports of the tornado described how wounded survivors received care in makeshift facilities.

Thus, a few weeks after the temporary emergency hospital closed, Mother Alfred approached Dr. Mayo with a visionary plan. The Sisters of Saint Francis would raise the funds to build a hospital and serve as nurses if he would agree to provide the medical and surgical care. Her plan seemed flawless. Dr. Mayo, however, was less than convinced. According to his later reflections, Dr. Mayo said:

…'Mother Superior, this city is too small to support a hospital.'…'Very well,' she persisted, 'but you just promise me to take charge of it and we will set that building before you at once. With our faith and hope and energy, it will succeed.'[33]

Finally, won over by Mother Alfred's conviction and no doubt inspired by her faith, Dr. Mayo agreed to the plan. For it to be realized, Mother Alfred's goal of building a hospital in the up-and-coming city would take determination, planning, and hard work. It would also take money, and for the next six years, the Franciscan Sisters sacrificed and saved to raise the funds. In the meantime, Mother Alfred worked closely with Dr. Mayo to choose the location of the hospital (nine acres just west of downtown Rochester), purchase the land, and hire a builder. In turn, Dr. W.W. Mayo, accompanied by his son, Dr. Will, toured

A native of Luxembourg, Mother Alfred Moes drew upon her religious faith and tenacious leadership skills in the founding of St. Mary's Hospital.

hospitals in the East to get the latest ideas about design and construction, meticulously planning a state-of-the-art facility.

The building plans called for a three-story, twenty-seven bed hospital:

It was to be constructed of red brick, with a large cross on top, window ledges of white, rough-hewn stone and four balconies on the north and west sides of the upper stories. The first floor would contain offices for three doctors, reception parlors, dining rooms and the kitchen. The operating room, women's wards and private rooms were located on the second floor, and the men's ward, recreation room and chapel on the third.[34]

As plans for the hospital moved forward, Charles Mayo received his medical degree from the Chicago Medical College (Northwestern University) on March 27, 1888. Another Rochester resident, Edith Maria Graham—daughter of Jane Graham—was in Chicago at the same time, studying nursing at Women's Hospital. In their own ways, Dr. W. W. Mayo, Dr. Will, Dr. Charlie, and Edith Graham were preparing to begin their historic collaboration with the Sisters of Saint Francis. Among the many outcomes of this dynamic partnership would be an internationally recognized model of excellence in nursing.

ENDNOTES

1 Jean Watson, *Nursing: Human Science and Human Care: A Theory of Nursing* (Sudbury, MA: Jones and Bartlett, 1999). See also Pamela Johnson, "Relationship-based Caring Model" (PowerPoint presentation, 31st International Association for Human Caring Conference Nursing Care Models, Mayo Clinic, Rochester, MN, June 2-5, 2010).

2 Susan Reverby, *Ordered to Care: The Dilemma of American Nursing, 1850-1945* (New York: Cambridge University Press, 1987): 11.

3 Clark Nelson, *Mayo Roots: Profiling the Origins of Mayo Clinic* (Rochester: Mayo Foundation for Medical Education and Research, 1990): 196-197.

4 For further reading on herbal medicine, see Martha M. Libster, *Herbal Diplomats: The Contribution of Early American Nurses (1830-1860) to Nineteenth-Century Health Care Reform and the Botanical Medical Movement* (West Lafayette, IN: Golden Apple Publications, 2004).

5 William Worrall Mayo, "Ledger entry, January 2, 1867," William Worrall Mayo's Ledger, Mayo Historical Unit, MHU-0666. While it is difficult to interpret his handwriting in this old ledger, most likely "opii" stood for "opium."

6 Louise Abigail Mayo, interview by Mrs. William B. Meloney, "Mrs. Mayo, Wilderness Mother," *The Delineator,* September 14, 1914. Reprint, Rochester: Mayo Family Public File, Olmsted County Historical Society.

7 Helen Clapesattle, *The Doctors Mayo* (Rochester: Mayo Foundation for Medical Education and Research, 1990): 95.

8 Meloney, *The Delineator.*

9 William Worrall Mayo, "Ledger entry, January 11, 1866," William Worrall Mayo's Ledger, Mayo Historical Unit, MHU-0666.

10 Nelson, *Mayo Roots,* 196-97.

11 Bruce Fye and Elizabeth Curry, *Teamwork at Mayo Clinic: An Experiment in Cooperative Individualism* (Rochester: Mayo Clinic Center for Humanities in Medicine, 2010).

12 Sister Ellen Whelan, *The Sisters Story: Saint Mary's Hospital-Mayo Clinic, 1889-1939* (Rochester: Mayo Foundation for Medical Education and Research, 2002): 9. See also Clapesattle, *The Doctors Mayo,* 25-26.

13 Charles H. Mayo, "Transitional Age in Medicine," *Proceedings of the Mayo Clinic, 7* (Rochester: Mayo Foundation for Medical Education and Research, 1932): 586-87.

14 Libster, *Herbal Diplomats,* 91.

15 The exception to the lack of trained nurses was the fact that some Catholic sisters and Lutheran deaconesses did nursing work out of their respective parishes. For further reading on this, see Barbra Mann Wall, *Unlikely Entrepreneurs: Catholic Sisters and the Hospital Marketplace, 1865-1925* (Columbus: The Ohio State University Press, 2005) and Lisa Zerull, "Nursing Out of the Parish: A History of the Baltimore Lutheran Deaconesses, 1893-1911" (dissertation, The University of Virginia, n.d.). See also Reverby, *Ordered to Care,* 23.

16 Reverby, *Ordered to Care,* 23.

17 Judith Hartzell, *Mrs. Charlie: The Other Mayo* (Gobles, MI: Arvi Books, 2000): 10.

18 William Worrall Mayo, "Ledger entry, January 1, 1867," William Worrall Mayo's Ledger, Mayo Historical Unit, MHU-0666.

19 Nelson, *Mayo Roots,* 20. See also Clapesattle, *The Doctors Mayo,* 3-37.

20 Nelson, *Mayo Roots,* 34.

21 Clapsattle, *The Doctors Mayo.*

22 W. Bruce Fye, "The Origins and Evolution of the Mayo Clinic from 1864 to 1939: A Minnesota Family Practice becomes an International 'Medical Mecca,'" *Bulletin of the History of Medicine, 84* (2010): 323-357.

23 Whelan, *Sisters Story,* 6.

24 Ibid., 39.

25 Ibid., 39.

26 "Rochester Tornado," *The Rochester Record & Union,* August 21, 1883. Reprint: Rochester. Mayo Historical Unit.

27 Whelan, *Sisters Story,* 39. See also Joseph Leonard, History of Olmsted County Minnesota (Chicago: Goodspeed Historical Association, 1910): 140-150 and "Rochester Tornado," *The Rochester Record & Union.*

28 St. Mary's School of Nursing-Senior Class of 1919, *St. Mary's Training School Annual,* 2nd ed. (Rochester: Hack & Wegner Ptg Co, 1919):1. Mayo Historical Unit, MHU-0676.

29 "The Origins and Development of Saint Marys," *St. Mary's School of Nursing (SMSN) Annual Report, 1920.* Mayo Historical Unit.

30 William W. Mayo, "Address," in *Memorial of St. Mary's Hospital,* (Rochester, Minnesota: St Mary's Hospital, 1894): 7-8. Mayo Historical Unit.

31 Barbra Mann Wall, *Unlikely Entrepreneurs: Catholic Sisters and the Hospital Marketplace, 1865-1925* (Columbus: The Ohio State University Press, 2005). From 1870 to 1920, Catholic sisters established 275 acute care hospitals across the country.

[32] Megan Malugani, Heritage Project, System Piece, p. 9.

[33] W. W. Mayo, "Address," 7-8.

[34] Philip K. Strand, *A Century of Caring, 1889-1989* (Rochester: Saint Marys Hospital, 1989).

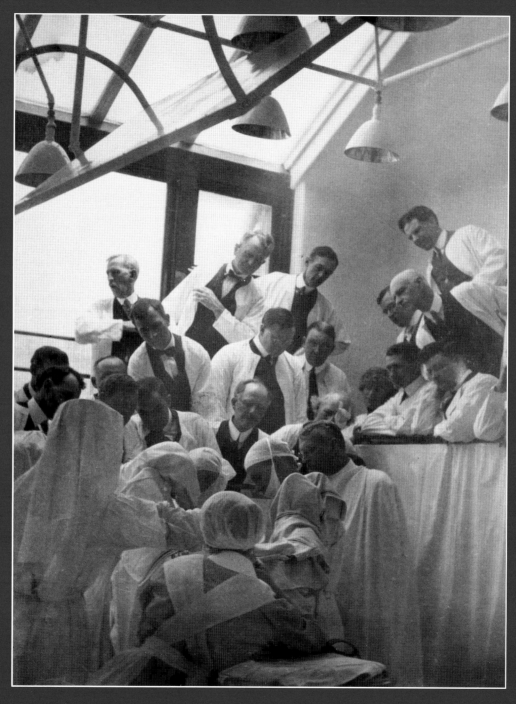

Sister Joseph Dempsey (far left) assisted Dr. William J. Mayo at St. Mary's Hospital. Visiting surgeons and nurses, who came to Rochester to learn from the Mayo brothers and their colleagues, crowded the observation gallery.

CHAPTER I

INTERLOCKING TALENTS

1889-1906

This drawing shows the original building of St. Mary's Hospital, which opened in 1889.

On September 30, 1889, the Sisters of Saint Francis had the new St. Mary's Hospital cleared of construction debris, scrubbed, outfitted with iron cots, and ready for a grand opening the next day.[1] That last day of September, however, several patients presented to the hospital, including a man who needed skin grafts on his leg and a patient in need of surgery for cancer of the eye. As a result, the Mayo doctors and Franciscan Sisters decided to open the hospital early. The decision to open early was a manifestation of a philosophy that Dr. Will had expressed in a 1910 address: "The best interest of the patient is the only interest to be considered."[2]

In the case of the patient with cancer of the eye, it was clear that the delicate procedure should take place in the new operating room. Its large skylight and bay window would illuminate the operating field, and its state-of-the-art operating table with adjustable headrest would be perfect for positioning the patient. Thus, the three Mayo physicians admitted both patients and proceeded directly to the operating room to perform surgery on the patient with cancer. In the operating room, the young Dr. Charlie, already known for his skill in eye, nose, and throat surgery, took the lead, assisted by his brother, Dr. Will. Their father, Dr. Mayo, gave the anesthesia.[3]

The next day, the formal opening of the hospital took place with Rochester's citizens, other visitors, and dignitaries attending the ceremonies. St. Mary's was typical of other modern hospitals being built throughout the United States in the latter half of the nineteenth century. In contrast to the almshouses that preceded them, the new hospitals, designed according to Florence Nightingale's recommendations, had sunlit, well-ventilated wards equipped with individual iron beds covered in clean linens. Since 1873, when the first Nightingale training schools for nurses opened in the United States, most hospitals had a cadre of well-disciplined student nurses who provided scientific care under the supervision of a trained graduate nurse.[4]

Reflecting this model, St. Mary's Hospital was neither a charity asylum for the poor nor a private home for the wealthy. Instead, it was a modern hospital that served all patients alike.[5] Within its walls, the talented Mayo physicians and nurses had access to a modern operating room where they treated patients using the latest surgical techniques. They also used Joseph Lister's theory of antisepsis (sterile surgery) to prevent infection. Following surgery, patients were transferred to clean, inviting wards where the Sisters of Saint Francis provided care.

This is not to say that St. Mary's Hospital in 1889 was modern in the present sense. When it opened, the hospital had minimal

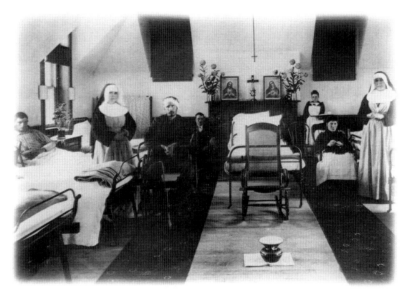

The Franciscan Sisters created a warm, welcoming environment. St. Mary's Hospital was open to everyone, regardless of race, creed, or ability to pay.

furnishings and even lacked many necessities. There were three wards and one private room for patients. About a dozen iron cots and some plain wooden chairs had been provided, along with three to four dozen unbleached muslin sheets and pillowcases and some gowns for the patients. A few quilts and some thin mattresses added to the small collection of supplies. Lanterns provided illumination at night; in fact, the Sisters hung one lantern from a tree in front of the hospital to guide physicians to the entrance.[6]

Rochester's First Professional Nurse

The spring before St. Mary's Hospital opened, Dr. Mayo had hired Edith Graham, R.N., a graduate of Women's Hospital Training School in Chicago and the only professionally educated nurse in Rochester, to be his "anesthetist, office nurse, general bookkeeper and secretary."[7] Edith Graham, the daughter of local midwife Jane Graham, returned to her hometown with excellent references attesting to her "unquestionable character, her scholarship and her industriousness." According to a letter of reference from J. H. Chapman, she had also proven to be a successful teacher—a quality that would soon serve her well in her work with the Sisters of Saint Francis.[8]

The intelligent and resourceful graduate of a good training school would bring sorely needed nursing expertise to St. Mary's Hospital, and her ability to share and disseminate knowledge would be especially important.[9] With the opening of the hospital in the autumn of 1889, Dr. W. W. Mayo needed Edith Graham to train the teaching Sisters of Saint Francis in specific nursing skills. His concept of "interlocking talents" for the good of the patient included everyone in the organization.[10] Collaboration and teamwork would be essential if the hospital was to run smoothly.

Under Edith Graham's tutelage, the Sisters would be well prepared for their nursing roles. Through lectures and demonstrations, she taught the Sisters how to take temperatures, check pulses, count respirations, apply flannel bandages, make beds, and administer medications. Teaching was only one aspect of her responsibilities at St. Mary's Hospital, however. She also kept medical records and cared for patients herself. In the operating room, Edith Graham saw to it that everything was ready for surgery and administered anesthesia. Following an operation, she closely assessed and monitored patients during their recovery.[11]

The Franciscan Sisters

Much as Edith Graham's skills were needed, the Franciscan Sisters would be essential to the hospital's success. After only a few weeks of instruction, the Sisters assumed the majority of the hospital nursing duties with a schedule that was rigorous. If a special nurse were

The daughter of a midwife, Edith Graham, R.N., was the first professionally educated nurse in Rochester. She taught nursing skills to the Franciscan Sisters when St. Mary's Hospital opened.

COLLABORATION

"In the hospital, Miss Graham was more than an anesthetist. She saw to it that everything was ready for surgery in the operating room, she administered the anesthetics to all surgical patients, and she remained with new surgical patients for part of the day."[12]

needed at night, a Sister stayed up and remained on duty until the next night. Two days and the night in between was not an unusual period on duty.[13]

Even without night duty, the days were long. In the late nineteenth century, carrying water, scrubbing floors and walls, making beds, serving patients' meals, and doing laundry were all included in the nurses' duties.[14] The fact that all the water used in the building had to be pumped by hand from a basement reservoir only added to the Sisters' work. At St. Mary's Hospital, there was only a crude elevator at first ("a sort of platform to be worked by means of ropes") and the Sisters carried water and patient meals up several flights of stairs.[15]

Mother Alfred herself often worked continuous shifts of one day and night and another day, lugging buckets of water, delivering trays of food to patients, shoveling coal, and pinking oilcloth to make covers for the washstands in the patients' rooms.[16]

In any hospital, laundry was a particularly demanding chore; at St. Mary's

To symbolize their friendship and mark each day of recovery, Sister Walburger Kululska and and her five-year-old patient, Lucy Ziok, made a new ring for the paper chain that decorated the hospital room.

Within a few weeks, Sister Joseph Dempsey arrived to help, followed the next year by Sister Sylvester Burke and Sister Fabian Halloran.[19] All were visionary leaders who could also get things done.[20]

Keen Observation

The Sisters were expected to be the eyes and hands of the physician, observing patients for changes in their conditions and skillfully carrying out the doctors' orders. Vigilant observation was critical to their work, as changes in the patient's color, skin turgor, pulse, or respiration could indicate a worsening or improving prognosis.

The Sisters soon became skilled at assessing their patients' conditions.

"Sister Fabian had the night watch on the surgical floors. If the telephone rang jarringly in the small hours of the morning, when sleep seemed most desirable, and Sister Fabian said that a patient was bleeding internally, it was best to throw on a gown and go at once, for she was seldom wrong in her diagnosis and never made a needless call."[21] The Sisters were also skilled in providing bedside care. One former patient wrote of their expertise:

the sheer volume of surgeries made that demand even higher. Operating room linen had to be washed, dried, and ironed in the evening so that it would be ready for use the next day.[17]

In addition to laundry and completing numerous other chores, the Sisters took time for daily devotions. Prayer was central to their mission of holistic care and became an essential element of nursing at St. Mary's. If the hospital Sisters were busy with patients or assisting in surgery, they asked others to pray. When a critical operation had to be done, the Sisters often asked the convent for prayers, and many a rosary was said to bless the surgeon's work during the operation.[18]

There were only four Sisters when the hospital opened: Sister Sienna Otto, Sister Constantine Koupal, Sister Fidelis Cashion, and Sister Hyacinth Quinlan.

THE ART OF HUMAN CONNECTION

"Sister Fabian greeted each of her patients with a kind word, then grasped their arm with a thin hand. By touching the patient's skin, she not only demonstrated her personal concern, but could immediately tell if they were feverish or chilled, or had a rapid pulse."

Being thoroughly schooled in surgical work, they are masters in the art of soothing and dressing wounds, of easing and succoring the wounded. They go about their work with a calmness and assurance born of an intimate

Alice McGaw, R.N. (far right), administered anesthesia
during a procedure performed by Dr. Will (third from right),
and his first assistant, Sister Joseph (second from right).
Alice McGaw became known as the "Mother of Nurse Anesthesia."

knowledge and patients generally affirm that this critical work is done with a minimum of discomfort and with a most delicate regard for their feelings and apprehensions. The duties incidental to surgical nursing are certainly performed in an artistic manner.[22]

Sister Fabian's use of touch to connect to her patients was legendary. She would, "greet each of her patients with a kind word, and then grasp their arm with a thin hand. By touching the patient's skin, she not only demonstrated her personal concern, but could immediately tell if they were feverish or chilled, or had a rapid pulse."[23]

During the first year that the hospital was open, the Drs. Mayo performed 300 operations. Some of these were pediatric surgeries, although there was no specific pediatric ward at the time. Indeed, anyone who needed care was admitted, regardless of age, ability to pay, race, gender, or religion. Mother Alfred Moes had made the Sisters' position clear, stating, "The cause of suffering humanity knows no religion and no sex; the charity of the Sisters of Saint Francis is as broad as their religion."[24]

Teamwork and Communication
Teamwork was important from the start. From 1889 to 1892, there were no male orderlies and the Mayo doctors themselves took responsibility of nursing male patients who needed special attention.[25]

Such cooperation became commonplace at St. Mary's; teamwork would be expected in the hospital where an experiment in cooperative individualism was taking place. As Dr. W.W. Mayo often said, no one "is big enough to be independent of others."[26]

Part of that interdependence required frequent communication between the Sisters and the Mayo physicians, and discussions often took place over informal meals in the hospital. At other times, communicating was more difficult. In the early years, the hospital had no telephone. When an emergency occurred and the Sisters needed the physicians, one of them left her work and carried the message on foot—a difficult task on the unpaved country roads, often with only lanterns to light the way at night. To address the problem, Dr. Mayo requested that the city set up telephone poles along the street from his home to the hospital, and the city complied.

Nurse Anesthetists
Shortly after Dr. W. W. Mayo hired Edith Graham, he taught her how to administer anesthesia using the open drop method a German physician had taught him a few years earlier.[27] Like other surgeons, Dr. Mayo had noticed that too often patients died from chloroform poisoning because the medical student or young physician assigned to give anesthesia would be so interested in watching the surgery itself

From the start, St. Mary's Hospital had state-of-the-art surgical equipment. Natural light helped illuminate this operating room.

that he would forget to watch the patient.[28] From his observations, Dr. Mayo concluded that a change in standard practice was necessary. Instead of having an inexperienced and inattentive medical student give anesthesia, he would delegate that responsibility to a specially trained nurse—in this case, one he had taught himself.

Under Dr. Mayo's direction, Edith Graham quickly became adept at using the open drop method of anesthesia delivery. The process was actually quite simple. A wire frame covered with gauze was placed over the patient's mouth and nose, and the anesthetizer would slowly place drops of the anesthetic agent on the cloth until the patient lost consciousness. The key was in vigilant observation of the patient's response to ensure that the patient neither suffocated nor came out of the anesthetized state.[29]

Between 1889 and 1893, the Mayos performed 655 surgical operations at St. Mary's Hospital. Of these, 98.3 percent were successful in that the patients left the hospital alive.[30] One of the key reasons for this success was that Edith Graham had given the anesthesia.

Edith Graham, R.N., used this equipment to administer anesthesia in the earliest surgical procedures at St. Mary's Hospital.

In 1893, Edith Graham retired from nursing when she married Dr. Charlie. That year, her friend, Alice Magaw, R.N., assumed her nursing responsibilities, administering anesthesia using the open drop method.[31] Later, publishing a review of 14,000 cases in which she had administered anesthesia, Alice Magaw was adamant that the open drop method had the best results:

In my series of cases, the 'open method' has been the method of choice. We have tried almost all methods advocated that seemed at all reasonable, such as nitrous oxide gas as a preliminary to ether (this method was used in 1,000 cases), a mixture of scopolamine and morphine as a preliminary to ether in 73 cases, also chloroform and ether, and have found them to be very unsatisfactory, if not harmful, and have returned to the 'drop method' each time, which method we have used for over 10 years.[32]

Both the method of delivering anesthesia and the level of skilled nursing care were essential to the patient's surviving the surgical procedure. It was equally important that the nurse anesthetist have a sound basis for her clinical judgment as well as an intentional therapeutic presence. For Alice Magaw, whom Dr. Charlie later dubbed "the Mother of Nurse Anesthesia," putting patients to sleep was an art as well as a science. The nurse anesthetist had to rely on her own observations, constantly monitoring the patient's pupils, skin color, pulse, muscle tone, and facial expression as well as the depth and effort of respirations in order to judge the patient's response and adjust the dosage of the anesthetic agent accordingly. As Alice Magaw explained:

The eyes give very early warning of danger. Some insist that the state of the pupils, the pulse or change in respiration is sure indication of danger, but to rely upon any one of these signs would be folly; carefully watch all of these symptoms, not relying on any one of them.[33]

Teaching

Teaching the art of anesthesia delivery was an important aspect of the Mayo nurse anesthetist's role, and Alice Magaw soon trained Mary Hines, R.N., to administer chloroform and ether. Her advice was sound: the nurse should inspire confidence in the patient, "talking him to sleep with the addition of as little ether as possible."[34]

Mary Hines learned quickly; she took over the service and became Dr. Will's anesthetist when Alice Magaw married and left the hospital. Later, during World War I, Mary Hines taught numerous Army nurses who came to Mayo Clinic for a six-week course in anesthesia delivery. By that time, Mayo Clinic was famous for its nurse anesthesia

In addition to serving as hospital superintendent, Sister Joseph was Dr. Will's first assistant. During surgery, with her small, delicate hands, she detected an abdominal growth that indicated cancer. "Sister Joseph's Nodule" became part of the medical literature.

training program, and nurse anesthetists were desperately needed on the Western Front.[35]

Sister Joseph Dempsey

Within a month of the hospital's opening in the fall of 1889, Mother Alfred called Sister Joseph Dempsey from the school in Kentucky where she was teaching and assigned her to St. Mary's. Under the direction of Edith Graham, Sister Joseph, a petite young woman with a ready smile, learned quickly and in six weeks she was made head nurse. Three years later, in 1892, she was appointed superintendent of the hospital.[36] Although modest and humble, Sister Joseph was a strong and effective leader, often deferring praise to the other Sisters.[37]

Until 1915, Sister Joseph served as first surgical assistant to Dr. Will. Noted for her attention to detail, clinical knowledge, and delicacy of touch, as well as her quiet demeanor and cooperative spirit, Sister Joseph became an essential member of the surgical team, contributing to the success of many most difficult operations.[38] She often anticipated the surgeon's needs, ready with the next instrument before it was requested.

It was said that if Dr. Will extended his hand and asked for instruments to begin closing the incision, and was instead handed a clamp by Sister Joseph, he automatically looked back into the incision, because it was likely that she had seen bleeding that he had missed.[39]

Clearly, Sister Joseph's vigilance in surgery was unmatched.

19

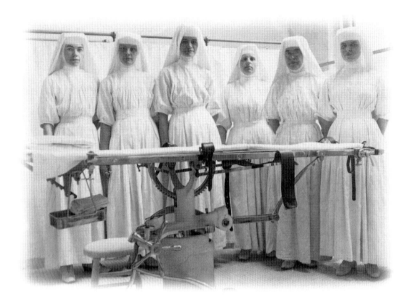

This photo shows operating room supervisors at St. Mary's Hospital. Beginning in 1920 with Sister William Fischenich, R.N. (third from left), supervisors developed postgraduate courses and wrote educational texts that helped establish Mayo's national reputation.

Nebraska, she was already familiar with the administration of ether and chloroform when she arrived in Rochester. She became expert under the watchful eye of Alice Magaw, refining her technique in the open drop method at St. Mary's. Like her mentor, Florence Henderson emphasized vigilant observation of the patient, writing that, "if the patient is carefully watched and not disturbed while doing well, the anesthetist will seldom meet with alarming conditions."[43]

St. Mary's Hospital Training School for Nurses

Except for the nurse anesthetists, until 1906, the Sisters were the only nurses at St. Mary's Hospital. However, as the Mayo brothers' reputation and the hospital continued to grow, teaching the next generation of nurses became necessary. In 1906, St. Mary's Hospital had 180 beds; that year 4,470 surgeries took place. By this time, the Mayo brothers had also added 20 physicians to their staff.[44] Chief among these were Augustus Stinchfield, M.D., Christopher Graham, M.D., Henry Plummer, M.D., Edward Starr Judd, M.D., and pathologist Louis Wilson, M.D.[45] With this growth came an ever-increasing demand for nurses.

Having coordinated three expansion projects for the hospital, Sister Joseph was concerned about the need for a nurse training program to prepare more nurses. Beds were of little use if there was no one to care for the patients.[46] Unprecedented numbers of patients and families were traveling to Rochester for state-of-the-art scientific care, and St. Mary's needed competent, trained nurses to provide it.[47] Before she could open a training program, however, Sister Joseph first

An Effective Team

With skilled assistants, modern techniques, and low patient mortality, the Mayos' reputation grew rapidly, and patients began to come from all parts of the state and beyond for treatment. Within three years, they were also coming from Iowa, Illinois, Kansas, Michigan, Missouri, Nebraska, North Dakota, New York, Ohio, South Dakota, and Wisconsin.[40] Soon St. Mary's had to increase both its bed capacity and personnel. As other surgeons joined the Mayo brothers, new operating rooms and additional nurse anesthetists were added. By 1903, St. Mary's had undergone three additions (in 1893, 1898, and 1903), making it one of the largest and most advanced hospitals in the United States.[41]

In 1904, Florence Henderson, R.N., joined the surgical team, replacing the departing physician anesthetist Isabella Herb, M.D.[42] Florence Henderson's expertise in the delivery of anesthesia was remarkable. As a member of the graduating class of 1900 from Bishop Clarkson Hospital Training School for Nurses in Omaha, had to find the right person to serve as the school's superintendent. In Rochester, there were few professional nurses who might qualify. Nonetheless, the fact that the Mayos' practice attracted numerous visitors—both physicians and nurses—provided Sister Joseph with an opportunity, and in 1906, she found the perfect director for the program. According to St. Mary's Annals:

In the gallery of the operating room one day, Sister Joseph observed a woman whose aspect and manner impressed her very favorably. Before leaving the OR, the woman introduced herself as Anna Jamme, told Sister of the work she had been doing in hospitals, and asked leave to see St. Mary's...[During the tour] when Jamme genuflected upon entering the chapel, Sister Joseph tentatively decided to engage her as superintendent of the training school ...[48]

Anna Jamme, R.N., a graduate of Baltimore's prestigious Johns Hopkins Training School for Nurses, proved to be an excellent choice, bringing knowledge of the basis of good nursing care, administrative ability, and vision to the new school.[49] She established a two-year nurse training program, mostly consisting of practical experience at the bedside, but also including twelve lectures in anatomy and physiology, attendance at eight post-mortem examinations, twelve lectures in bacteriology, and six classes in sanitation and hygiene.

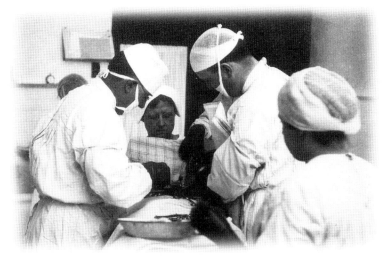

Florence Henderson, R.N. (second from left), refined the technique of open drop anesthesia.

GUARDIAN FOR PATIENT SAFETY

"If the patient is carefully watched and not disturbed while doing well, the anesthetist will seldom meet with alarming conditions."

FLORENCE HENDERSON, R.N.

In addition, the program included lectures on medical-surgical diseases and dietetics, along with several classes in practical nursing.[50] Teaching, in the classroom and on the wards, would clearly be part of the nurses' role at St. Mary's Hospital.

On November 19, 1906, Sister Joseph formally opened St. Mary's Hospital Training School for Nurses. The school's opening was timely. In just the next decade, Mayo Clinic would be officially named; additional hospitals and another nursing school would be added to the growing medical complex in Rochester; and a world war and an influenza pandemic would bring unexpected new challenges. The demand for nurses would only increase.

Starting in 1906, Anna Jamme, R.N., served as first superintendent of St. Mary's Hospital Training School for Nurses.

21

This painting depicts an early procedure at St. Mary's Hospital. From left, Sister Constantine Koupal,
Dr. W.W. Mayo, Dr. Charlie, Edith Graham, R.N., Dr. Will, and Sister Joseph Dempsey.
Dr. Charlie built the operating table.

Mother Alfred Moes

Sister Joseph Dempsey

Sister Sienna Otto

Sister Fidelis Cashion

Sister Constantine Koupal

Sister Sylvester Burke

Sister Fabian Halloran

ENDNOTES

Chapter title from Charles Mayo, *Mayo: The Story of My Family and My Career* (Garden City, Doubleday, 1968): 23.

1 Helen Clapesattle, *The Doctors Mayo* (Rochester: Mayo Foundation for Medical Education and Research, 1990): 142.

2 William J. Mayo, "The Necessity of Cooperation in the Practice of Medicine" (commencement address, Rush Medical College, Chicago, IL, June 15, 1910), in *Collected Papers of St. Mary's Hospital* (Rochester, 1910): 557-566. Mayo Historical Unit.

3 Sister Mary Brigh, "Medical History in Minnesota: A Symposium" (paper read at the 57th Annual Meeting of the Medical Library Association, Rochester, MN, June 2-6, 1958): 25.

4 For more on this topic, see Patricia D'Antonio, *American Nursing: A History of Knowledge, Authority, and the Meaning of Work* (Baltimore: The Johns Hopkins University Press, 2010).

5 Sister Ellen Whelan, *The Sisters Story: Saint Mary's Hospital-Mayo Clinic, 1889-1939* (Rochester, MN: Mayo Foundation for Medical Education and Research, 2002): 50.

6 "Hardships of the Early Days": 23. Reprint: Rochester. Mayo Historical Unit.

7 Jean Pougiales, "The First Anesthetizers at the Mayo Clinic," *Journal of the American Association of Nurse Anesthetist,* 38, no. 3 (1970): 235-241.

8 J.H. Chapman, recommendation letter for Edith Graham, August 14, 1887. Mayo Historical Unit, Edith Graham Collection, MHU-0735, Box 001.

9 Edith Graham, lecture notes in Edith Graham's notebook, n.d. Mayo Historical Unit, original in Olmsted County Historical Society, Box 001.

10 Charles Mayo, *Mayo: The Story of My Family and My Career* (Garden City: Doubleday, 1968): 23.

11 Pougiales, "First Anesthetizers," 235-241.

12 Ibid.

13 Whelan, *Sisters Story,* 66.

14 For further reading on this, see Susan Reverby, *Ordered to Care: The Dilemma of American Nursing, 1850-1945* (Cambridge: Cambridge University Press, 1987).

15 "Hardships of the Early Days": 23.

16 Marianne L. Hockema, "The Franciscan Five Saint Marys Hospital's Sister Administrators" (Presentation, 2002): 1-41; quote, 13-14.

17 Whelan, *Sisters Story,* 66.

18 Ibid., 67.

19 Ibid., 59.

20 Jane Campion, "Sisters Story Interviews," 2010, transcript: 1-17.

21 Chapter VIII: "The Trained Nurse": 76. Reprint: Rochester. Mayo Historical Unit.

22 "Reminiscences of Saint Marys" (1919): 1-5; quote, 4. Reprint: Rochester. Mayo Historical Unit, Saint Marys School of Nursing archives.

23 *A Century of Caring,* p. 24. See also Pamela Johnson, "The Art of Human Connection" (PowerPoint presentation, 2010).

24 Hockema, "The Franciscan Five," 12.

25 Whelan, *Sisters Story,* 66.

26 William Worrall Mayo, M.D. See also Fye and Curry, *Teamwork at Mayo Clinic,* 2 (see Prologue, n. 11).

27 Pougiales, "First Anesthetizers," 236.

28 Judith Hartzell, *Mrs. Charlie, The Other Mayo* (Gobles, MI: Arvi Books, 2000): 17.

29 Arlene Keeling, "Prescribing Medicine without a License?: Nurse Anesthetists, 1900-1938," in *Nursing and the Privilege of Prescription* (Columbus Ohio: Ohio State University Press, 2007).

30 Pougiales, "First Anesthetizers," 236.

31 American Association of Nurse Anesthetists, www.aana.com/archives/timeline.asp (accessed January 16, 2005; site now discontinued). Magaw was so skilled in her technique, that years later, Charles Mayo named her "the Mother of Anesthesia" for her mastery of open-drop ether administration.

32 Alice Magaw, "A Review of Over 14,000 Surgical Anesthesias," *Surgery, Gynecology, and Obstetrics* (December 1906): 795.

33 Alice Magaw, "Observations of 1092 Cases of Anesthesia from January 1, 1899- January 1, 1900," *The St. Paul Medical Journal,* 2 (May 1900): 307.

34 Magaw, "A Review," 795-799.

35 Mary Sarnecky, *A History of the U.S. Army Nurse Corps* (Philadelphia: University of Pennsylvania Press, 1999).

36 Sister Mary Brigh Cassidy, "Sister Mary Joseph" (1960): 1-3. Mayo Historical Unit, Dempsey File, MHU #0675.

37 Clark Nelson, "Historical Profiles of Mayo: 100th Anniversary of Sister Mary Joseph Dempsey," *Mayo Clinic Proceedings,* 67 (1992): 512. Mayo Historical Unit, Dempsey File, MHU #0675.

38 William J. Mayo, "A Tribute from William J. Mayo," *A Souvenir of Saint Mary's Hospital,* 57; see also Nelson, "Historical Profiles of Mayo," 512.

39 Hockema, "Franciscan Five," 18.

40 "A Souvenir of Saint Mary's Hospital": 16. Reprint: Rochester. Mayo Historical Unit.

41 Whelan, *Sisters Story,* 102; see also Twenty-Ninth Annual Report, (1918): 11. Mayo

Historical Unit.

42   Joan Hunziker-Dean, "Voice and Touch: Florence Henderson on the Skills of an Ether Specialist," *AANA Journal,* 67 (1999): 263-269.

43   Florence Henderson, "Ether Anesthesia," *The St Paul Medical Journal,* 16, 2 (1914): 74-81.

44   Whelan, *Sisters Story,* 102.

45   Ibid., 84.

46   Nelson, "Historical Profiles of Mayo," 512. Mayo Historical Unit, Dempsey File, MHU #0675.

47   Sister Mary Brigh, "Medical History in Minnesota" (June 2-6, 1958).

48   "The Seed is Sown": 1. Reprint: Rochester. Mayo Historical Unit, Folder "For 50 Years: Going Forth to Serve."

49   Ibid., 1.

50   Ibid., 1.

Anna Jamme, R.N., (first row, second from right) was the original superintendent of the St. Mary's Hospital Training School for Nurses, pictured here with graduates of the first two classes (1908 and 1909).

CHAPTER II

A UNIQUE SISTERHOOD

1907-1939

Members of the classes of 1908, 1909, and 1910 participated in the first commencement ceremony of the St. Mary's Hospital Training School for Nurses.

With Anna Jamme and her successors at the helm, St. Mary's Hospital Training School for Nurses thrived, preparing hundreds of nurses over the years, not only Catholic sisters but also lay women. During their training, St. Mary's students formed "a unique sisterhood"—one that expressed an organizational culture that later would be called the Mayo Mystique and, later still, the Mayo Clinic Model of Care.[1]

This culture drew upon the taproot values of the Sisters of Saint Francis but also included other influences.[2] For example, graduates of the Colonial Hospital Training School for Nurses, and the schools that evolved from it, also became members of that unique community, for they, too, shared the experience of training and working in hospitals associated with Mayo Clinic. In time, the presence of men in nursing would shift the gender-specific focus of the sisterhood, while emphasizing the unique professional attributes of Mayo Clinic nursing.

Starting in the early 1900s, two major factors contributed to the unique identity of the Rochester nurses: 1) the distinctive setting in which they worked and 2) the opportunities to learn that were inherent in it. Rochester nurses had the advantage of using state-of-the-art medicines and equipment almost as soon as each was available. At the turn of the twentieth century, these included drugs such as aspirin and digitalis, x-ray machines, electrocardiographs, and suction apparatus. By the mid-1920s, special shipments of insulin, the newly discovered treatment for diabetes mellitus came to Mayo Clinic from Toronto, and oxygen chambers were installed for use with patients.[3]

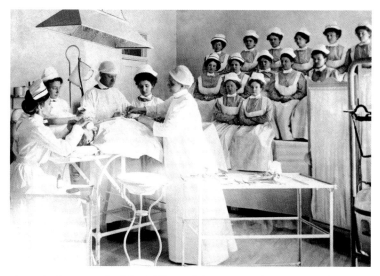

A surgical team at St. Mary's Hospital demonstrated operative techniques for nursing school students, circa 1913.

In addition to having access to state-of-the-art medical treatments, nurses benefited from working, learning, and researching with the medical staff. The Mayo brothers, along with the physicians and scientists who joined them, valued education in every aspect of patient care, from the operating rooms to the wards. As school of nursing instructor Elsie Krug, R.N., recalled, "Dr. Will and Dr. Charlie were very real personalities for us all."[4] In many ways, the nurses' learning opportunities had a positive effect on staff recruitment and retention and they had more opportunities to learn at St. Mary's than elsewhere.[5]

By 1914, St. Mary's Hospital Training School for Nurses had lengthened its program to three years; the next year the State Board of Examiners accredited it.[6] The accreditation decision was not

surprising. The student nurses' experiences at St. Mary's Hospital were amazing. Students saw all types of illness, disease, and surgical procedures numerous times, and worked with world-renowned medical specialists and surgeons, learning not only expert scientific care but also the art of nursing with its focus on holistic patient care.[7]

That focus on holistic care also included attention to a healthy lifestyle for the nurses themselves. In Rochester, students benefited from a wide variety of extracurricular activities, all designed to prepare them to be well-rounded, healthy professional nurses. Teas, swimming events, picnics, church attendance, canoeing, and concerts filled their off-duty hours.[8] Elsie Krug, recalled an experience that was a highlight for many nurses, "Dr. Will invited each class for a day on his yacht, the *North Star*. This meant a ride on the Mississippi and a carry-along chicken dinner provided by the Sisters."[9]

Sister Paul Conely, R.N., (first row, far right) along with other Franciscan Sisters, enjoyed a trip aboard the North Star *with Dr. Will and his wife, Hattie.*

28

In the clinical setting and in the classroom, as well as during social events, St. Mary's nursing students had advantages far exceeding those in other hospitals.[10] News of their exceptional education spread, and additional young women soon began to apply for admission to the school. The increase in applications came at the right time. As the twentieth century opened, patients were coming to Rochester in ever increasing numbers. Between 1908 to 1912, patient registration jumped approximately 300 percent, and professional nurses were needed to care for them.[11]

Growth of the Clinic

With the growth of the Mayos' practice and the increase in the number of medical professionals in Rochester, the town needed hotel space, additional hospital beds, and new residences for the nurses.

To address those needs, in 1906, the John H. Kahler Corporation, formed to build not only lodging but also hospitals, and purchased and remodeled a large private home near the Mayos' office, opening in 1907 as the first Kahler Hotel.[12] This unique facility reflected the Mayos' longstanding focus on holistic care for patients and families. As a local newspaper reported, the Kahler Hotel had "the novel aspect of being a home, a hospital, a sanatorium and an infirmary, all in one."[13] Under the auspices of the Kahler Corporation, additional hospitals, some combined with hotel accommodations, would be built in downtown Rochester.

Having enough housing for the nurses was also important, and in 1912, "a magnificent Nurses Home was built so nursing students no longer would have to live over the laundry in St. Mary's Hospital or board in private homes.[14]

Kahler Hall (left) provided housing for students in the downtown nursing school. Marian Hall (right) was the dormitory for students of the nursing school at St. Mary's Hospital.

By the early 1920s, St. Mary's Hospital was one of the nation's largest private hospitals.

New additions to *existing* buildings also increased the number of hospital beds in Rochester and provided the opportunity to allocate specific wards to different medical specialties. By 1912, St. Mary's Hospital had added a 5-story south wing, expanding its capacity to 300 beds and 6 operating rooms. The fifth floor of the new wing, set aside for maternity patients, would be well utilized.[15] In the early twentieth century, with the Progressive Era attention to maternal/infant mortality and the emphasis on the importance of having physicians and professional nurses to attend births, more women were choosing to deliver their babies in hospitals rather than at home.[16]

This pin, circa 1925, was a distinctive emblem of the St. Mary's Training School for Nurses. The school's name went through several changes in its history, ultimately becoming known as Saint Marys School of Nursing.

In 1912, besides the maternity ward, St. Mary's Hospital opened a ward devoted to pediatrics. Since 1895, Christopher Graham, M.D., had been seeing most of the pediatric patients, along with, beginning in 1906, Herbert Giffin, M.D. By 1911, the two had formed a Subsection Responsible for the Care of Children, and now, a year later, would have a pediatric ward staffed by nurses specifically dedicated to that care.[17]

The First Mayo Clinic Building

On October 9, 1912, the Mayo brothers and their partners laid the cornerstone of the first Mayo Clinic building—designed to be a permanent house in which scientific investigation could take place and where every effort could be made to cure the sick and suffering.[18]

After two years of construction, the Mayo Clinic building was completed, and on March 6, 1914, Rochester's citizens thronged to its opening. The building was designed to promote an environment of healing.[19] Business offices, registration desks, examining rooms, x-ray cubicles, laboratories, a library, editorial offices, and an art studio completed the facility.[20] The spacious lobby, decorated with wicker furniture and a fountain banked with palms, offered a stark contrast to the old hallway waiting room and would set the stage for a focus on holistic care for patients.[21]

The opening of the new Clinic building was significant; it marked the end of the "office period" in which no distinguishing feature set the Mayos' practice apart from that of any other group of office-based physicians and surgeons.[22] It also marked the emergence of Mayo Clinic as a distinct institution that was independent of any hospital and was the building in which patients were initially seen for diagnosis and treatment.[23]

ENVIRONMENT

The lobby of the clinic building, in "stark contrast to the old hallway waiting room," would set the stage for a focus on holistic care for patients.[23]

Its central tenet, based on the Mayo brothers' longstanding values, was "cooperative group practice."[24] That precept of cooperation was not reserved exclusively for physicians. From the start, a spirit of cooperation and collaboration pervaded the entire Clinic and its personnel, including, of course, the nurses. For many patients, interaction with the nurse who took them into an examining room, checked their vital signs, and listened to their troubles was their first experience at the famous Mayo Clinic.

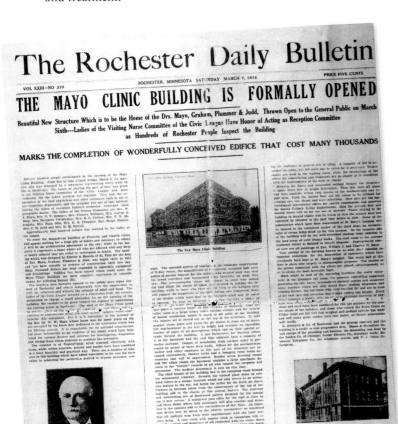

The Mayo brothers opened an outpatient building with facilities for patient care, education, and research in 1914.

31

Dermatology Nursing

A spirit of cooperation and collaboration also pervaded the hospitals affiliated with Mayo Clinic. One example was evident in the new clinical section of Dermatology and Syphilology organized by John Stokes, M.D., in 1916. First providing care at Colonial Hospital and later in the Worrall Annex, the service offered unique experiences for nurses to collaborate with physicians.[25] Indeed, nurses, rather than physicians, spent numerous hours caring for patients, assessing the condition of their skin, and administering complicated dermatologic therapies including oatmeal baths and applications of ointments and creams.[26] The nurses also provided psychological support. According to Supervisor Arlene Crepps, R.N., the dermatology nurse had to have "a fundamental knowledge of psychology [to care for] the mind as well as the body."[27] Above all, the dermatology nurse was to keep the patient comfortable. If the prescribed treatment was "not soothing," it was necessary that "it be changed as quickly as possible."[28] In an article titled "The Art of Dermatologic Nursing," Arlene Crepps wrote, "A good dermatology nurse can insure her patient fifty percent of his cure and ninety percent of his comfort."[29]

Nurses played a key role in establishing dermatology as a specialty at Mayo Clinic. Staff members gathered for this photograph around 1917.

SCIENCE OF HEALTH CARE

"A good dermatology nurse can insure her patient fifty percent of his cure and ninety percent of his comfort."

ARLENE CREPPS, R.N.

Beyond the Clinic Walls

The Mayo spirit of cooperation spread beyond the walls of the Clinic and its affiliated hospitals in Rochester. Starting in 1883, when the Sisters of Saint Francis provided nursing to survivors of the tornado, caring for the larger community had been a core value at St. Mary's Hospital.

One episode in the winter of 1916 demonstrates that commitment. Infected cow milk caused an epidemic to sweep through the small town of Galesville, Wisconsin. The infection took different forms in different people. For some it was septic sore throat, in others, erysipelas (a severe skin rash accompanied by fever and vomiting, caused by streptococci bacteria) of a most virulent form.[30] Many people had already died. Others were dying. Martha Schuman, R.N., one of three nurses from St. Mary's to go to Galesville in a blinding snowstorm, recalled:

When we arrived...we were met by a team and a bob sleigh and driven to one of the physician's offices where we received orders...I was sent to a case supposedly three and a half miles out, but it was really twice as far. I found four people very sick and later two more developed the disease. A boy of 16 years had been at school in town and brought home a quart of milk...and the family all...became infected. A girl, 18 years old, was in a dying condition when I arrived...temperature 104.6 F. and suffering great pain. A grandmother 76 had erysipelas...these two were in beds in the parlor...In a small adjoining room were the two boys, 16 and 12 years...Having my orders, I tried to do what I could and soon had them more comfortable.[31]

It would not be the last time nurses from Rochester would respond to a crisis in another town. In the years to come, the presence of a team from Mayo Clinic would be a common sight during regional and national disasters.

The Colonial Hotel-Hospital

As the Mayos' reputation continued to grow, so did the need for facilities in Rochester, and new hospitals appeared in rapid succession. With them came an ever-increasing need for nurses.

In March 1916, the Colonial Hotel-Hospital opened, at first serving as a hotel-hospital for convalescent patients. There, under the direction of Superintendent of Nurses Mary Gill, R.N., graduate nurses provided the nursing care. Using nurses that have graduated to provide bedside care was unique at the time. In most hospitals throughout the United States, student nurses, an inexpensive and disciplined

workforce, worked in hospital wards, while most graduate nurses worked outside the hospital as private duty nurses.[32] When it opened, however, Colonial Hospital did not have a training school, so there were no student nurses who could staff the wards. This lack of a student workforce would soon become a problem. With the United States' entry into World War I in 1917, many of Colonial's nurses left to serve in military camps and hospitals at home and abroad, leaving the hospital significantly understaffed. This experience was part of a national trend; almost 9,000 nurses volunteered with the Army and Navy Nurse Corps, creating a serious shortage of nurses in civilian hospitals throughout the country.[33] Responding to this shortage, Colonial's leaders, Chief of Staff Melvin Henderson, M.D., and Mary Gill, recommended the establishment of a school of nursing. The two-year program opened in September 1918 as the Colonial Hospital Training School for Nurses, providing a new source of labor for the hospital.[34]

Colonial Hospital used this ambulance to serve patients.

Preparation for War

Even before the United States entered the war, Surgeon General of the United States, Rupert Blue, M.D., had requested that the U.S. medical community prepare for the possibility. To lead the endeavor, he appointed Dr. Will as Chairman of the Committee of American Physicians for Medical Preparedness and had named Dr. Charlie as a member.

Under Dr. Will's leadership, the committee established a medical reserve corps and outlined a plan to organize fifty base hospitals that could be deployed to Europe should the need arise. Each base hospital would be located fifty miles behind the front lines of battle. Each would be staffed by 27 medical officers, 60 nurses, and 153 enlisted men. Staff, funds, and supplies would be donated by large hospitals and medical schools.[35] Under this plan, the University of Minnesota and Mayo Clinic organized Base Hospital 26.

In the spring of 1917, shortly after the United States declared war on Germany, Dr. Will and Arthur Law, M.D., Associate Professor of Surgery at the University of Minnesota, began the organization

Courtesy Library of Congress

Many women answered the call to serve their country as nurses in World War I. Red Cross volunteer nurses held a march in Rochester to support the war effort.

Dr. Will (left) and Dr. Charlie worked with the U.S. Surgeon General during World War I. Both brothers were commissioned as brigadier generals in the Medical Reserve Corps of the U.S. Army.

process. Raising funds would be the first priority. The Mayo brothers contributed $15,000 of the $30,000 goal for Base Hospital 26. Their contribution was significant; it was essentially one-quarter of the $60,000 combined total raised by the American Red Cross, private citizens, the University of Minnesota, and others.[36] As a result, when it departed for France in June 1918, the Mayo Unit or Minnesota Unit (as Base Hospital 26 would soon become known), would have not only an eminently qualified staff of physicians and nurses, but also the best available equipment. The journal *Military Surgeon* reported:

A letter recently reached the American Red Cross headquarters in Washington from Dr. William J. Mayo of Rochester, Minnesota, stating his willingness to organize a base hospital...An American soldier will be indeed fortunate who falls into the hands of this unit.[37]

LEADERSHIP

"A letter recently reached the American Red Cross headquarters in Washington from Dr. William J. Mayo of Rochester, Minnesota, stating his willingness to organize a base hospital... An American soldier will be indeed fortunate who falls into the hands of this unit."

Florence Bullard, R.N.

Even before the base hospitals were mobilized, some American nurses volunteered to go overseas, serving alongside British and French nurses.[38] Among them was Florence Bullard, R.N., a St. Mary's Hospital nurse who left for the battlefields of Europe in December 1916.[39] Writing on September 26, 1917, to her friends back home, she described her situation:

I am at a base hospital near to the war zone, near enough so you can hear the cannon roaring all the time...Tomorrow we start for the first place where it is possible to operate behind the trenches. There are sixteen surgeons...I am the only nurse going in this group and I am assigned to the chief surgeon. Other army nurses are coming next week...I realize since yesterday that this is no child's play...I shall have to wear a gas mask several hours a day and be in constant range of the big guns. The operating room with which I am connected is in a traveling automobile... The cases are cared for a few hours and then the ambulance and stretcher bearers carry them to the first aid hospital...[40]

As thousands of wounded flooded the triage centers on the front lines—

some to be patched up and moved on, some to be operated on immediately—Florence Bullard's previous experience in Rochester would serve her well. First containing trauma and then paying attention to hygiene and infection control, she worked tirelessly, dressing wounds and assisting surgeons—sometimes in hospital

cellars where there was no daylight, the cots so close together she could just get between them.[41] In one letter home, she commented on the sheer volume of injured soldiers who presented for care at her medical unit, noting that "...all day and night, [new ones arrived] as fast as others were out."[42] Patient survival was the priority, followed by promoting comfort. Florence Bullard and her colleagues helped stop hemorrhaging, dressed and re-dressed wounds, and offered the soldiers feedings of beef-tea, rice-water, and milk. They also administered small amounts of morphine for pain relief—too much would cause circulatory collapse.[43]

In spite of bombings and tremendous stress, Florence Bullard never wavered. On September 4, 1918, she was awarded the Croix de Guerre (War Cross) with Bronze Star by the French government for bravery during the war.

Nurse Anesthetists as Teachers

Back home, nurse anesthetists at St. Mary's Hospital were serving their country by teaching anesthesia administration techniques to a long succession of trainees.[44] With the shortage of surgeons at the Front, U.S. military leaders recognized that they needed more nurse anesthetists to free up surgeons to operate. As a result, the Army sent

Florence Bullard, R.N., received high honors from the French government for her heroism during World War I by providing exemplary nursing care under combat conditions.

Left: Nurses who received this and other types of specialized training were equipped to meet the demands of wartime medicine. Below: Under the leadership of Mary Hines, R.N., the nurse anesthesia program at St. Mary's Hospital earned national acclaim.

groups of twenty nurses at a time to Rochester to study the art and science of anesthesia. Of the few nurse anesthesia programs then available, the program at St. Mary's Hospital, under the supervision of Mary Hines, R.N., was considered one of the best in the United States.[45]

By 1917, St. Mary's Hospital had six operating rooms, each staffed with a first and second assistant, an anesthetist, a graduate head nurse, and a student nurse. Combined with the fact that surgeries took place six days a week, there were plenty of opportunities to learn.[46] Ordinarily, training consisted of several months of apprenticeship in the practical and the theoretical aspects of the work.[47] Under

wartime circumstances, however, the course lasted only six weeks. It was important to get the new nurse anesthetists back to the Front as soon as possible.[48]

During the first week in Minnesota, the Army nurses merely observed the activities of a regular anesthetist in the operating room. They then gradually assumed the anesthetist's responsibilities...the students continued doing more until they had total charge of the patient's anesthesia...The goal was to have the Army nurse administer anesthesia to fifty patients... on her own...before she left.[49]

WHITE STAR LINE
TWIN-SCREW R.M.S. "BALTIC."

A converted passenger ship, the R.M.S. Baltic, conveyed Mayo Clinic personnel to war-torn Europe in 1918.

The Mobilization of Base Hospital 26

Over the summer of 1917, the Mayo doctors and their colleagues from the University of Minnesota continued to assemble staff and equipment for Base Hospital 26. After waiting all fall, on December 10, 1917, the unit received orders to depart for South Carolina for training. From there they moved to New Jersey to prepare for deployment. Finally, in June 1918, Base Hospital 26 received orders to embark for Europe.

On June 4, 1918, Base Hospital 26 nurses, under the charge of Chief Nurse Annie Gosman, R.N., sailed with the unit on the Royal Mail Ship (R.M.S.) *Baltic.* To avoid torpedoes, the ship zigzagged its way across the Atlantic.[50] After landing in Liverpool twelve days later, the group from Base Hospital 26 traveled by train to the French village of Allerey.[51] St. Mary's alumna May MacGregor Givens, R.N., documented her experience on that trip:

...The nurses were assigned six to each compartment...with knees touching. We slept as best we could—sitting up...We stopped from time to time at Red Cross stations for what conveniences they could offer. Before leaving, we were each handed a can of jam through the window. That jam,

added to what we had left from our lunch box, was our food for the next three day...We were three days and three nights on the way. When we arrived, we were exhausted.[52]

TEAMWORK

"...The ten nurses who had come from St. Mary's at Rochester were all assigned to Mobile #1. This, we learned, was because of our surgical experience...We were bound together as sisters by our common background..."

In Allerey, there would be no rest. On arrival, the nurses immediately set up camp and began preparations for the expected onslaught of the wounded.

Mobile Hospital 1

Not all of the nurses would stay in Allerey with Base Hospital 26. Within a few days, several were dispatched to Mobile Hospital 1 in Coulomniers, a small village thirty-five miles from Paris toward the German lines, where they treated injured soldiers before sending them to base hospitals farther from the Front.[53]

...The ten nurses who had come from St. Mary's at Rochester were all assigned to Mobile #1. This, we learned, was because of our surgical experience...We were bound together as sisters by our common background...[54]

The receiving unit of Base Hospital 26 treated about 7,200 soldiers. A nurse wrote, "Everything was sacrificed to speed up the handling of the hundreds of boys lying on the ground at the front lines."

...the most pitiful thing...was to step outside the hospital tents and see hundreds of stretchers on the ground, each bearing a man who must wait probably for hours before he could be taken care of. We had 17 operating tables working day and night and yet we could not keep up with the work.[57]

In Coulomniers, a constant stream of wounded arrived directly from the trenches of Chateau-Thierry, an area of significant fighting.[55] Writing back to her colleagues in Rochester, May MacGregor Givens, recounted a typical day:

...The wounded by the hundreds were taken in on litters by corpsmen...the seriously wounded were kept at the mobile hospital...We prepared them quickly for surgery, cutting away their blood soaked clothing...As routine, we gave hypodermic injections to combat infection...Everything was sacrificed to speed up the handling of the hundreds of boys lying on the ground at the front lines...sorting of the most urgently injured, and amputating whenever necessary came to be a routine we accomplished with speed and without words, often in near darkness, always with the noise of exploding bombs...in our ears.[56]

Nurse anesthetist Sophie Gran Jevne Winton, R.N., also recalled those days, writing:

Writing home to her colleagues, Winifred Ashba, R.N., confirmed the enormity of the nurses' task, "...I will say this: all the operating room lists at the various hospitals back in Rochester put together would seem tame in comparison..."[58] Writing to her sister on July 23, 1918, St. Mary's Hospital nurse

Base Hospital 26: "We had 17 operating tables working day and night and yet we could not keep up with the work."

Nell Bryant, R.N., served with "the Mayo Unit" in France. She and her colleagues were commended for their service during some of America's heaviest fighting in the war.

from the Mayo brothers had not arrived. As a result, the unit had to turn to the American Red Cross for the donation of many special instruments and supplies of bath robes, pajamas, bed socks, and more.[61] A few weeks later, when the first hospital trains pulled into Allerey on July 23, 1918, things were still "more or less in a topsy-turvy state" and the entire staff, including the nurses, had to improvise to care for the injured men.[62] In the end, biscuit tins were used for sinks, tubs, and in the laboratory.[63] It was Mayo problem solving at its best.

anesthetist Nell Bryant, R.N., described the overwhelming amount of work, "We have been so rushed since the big drive began; we hardly have time to sleep or eat!"[59]

Nell Bryant and the other nurses of Mobile Hospital 1 would later be cited for bringing comfort and assistance to the wounded during the St. Mihel and Meuse-Argonne campaigns.[60] Nurses affiliated with Mayo Clinic demonstrated a powerful sense of duty, teamwork, and caring, as well as the ability to adapt to rapidly changing circumstances.

Problem Solvers
While some of their group worked all summer and into the fall of 1918 with Mobile Hospital 1, other nurses who had embarked for Europe with Base Hospital 26 remained in Allerey from the day they arrived.

Unfortunately, the sophisticated equipment and supplies Base Hospital 26 had purchased in the United States with generous funding

A powerful sense of mission and teamwork inspired the nurses of Base Hospital 26. When the wounded arrived and supplies were short, they improvised to meet the needs of each patient.

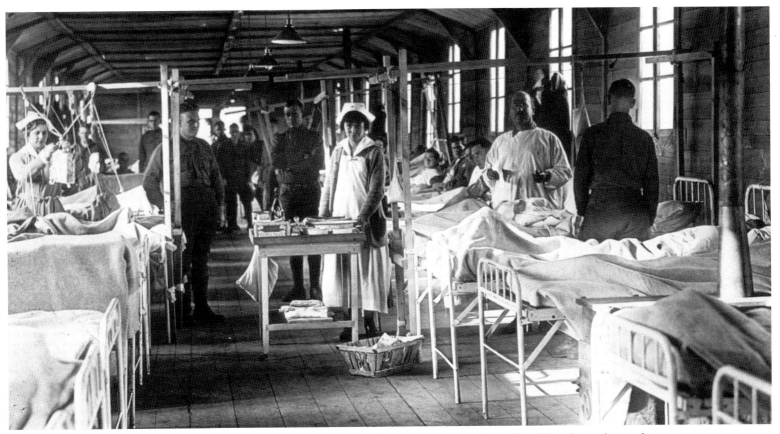

Nurses adapted to serving patient needs that could scarcely be imagined in civilian life—shrapnel wounds, horrific burns, trench-borne infections, and the effects of poison gas.

Throughout the summer of 1918, wounded soldiers streamed into Allerey every day, many with gruesome shrapnel wounds infected from days in muddy trenches. Others presented with burns from head to toe, and lungs destroyed by mustard gas. When hundreds of casualties arrived from the Chateau-Thierry region, 398 patients were admitted to Base Hospital 26. A second convoy came on July 30, "transferred from overcrowded and overworked evacuation hospitals...[Then], four operating room tables were arranged and two surgical teams worked at the same time."[64] May MacGregor Givens, R.N., wrote:

We learned quickly what to do. Our first job was to cut away the clothing. This had to be done as quickly as possible, for enough of the wicked gas was usually enmeshed in the fibers to burn deeper and deeper into the flesh. We each had a long, bent scissors for this purpose. We had to stand as far away as possible from the patient, for the fumes from the clothing could also be dangerous to us.[65]

Base Hospital 26 soon filled to its capacity of 2,000 patients. Distribution of the 65 nurses to provide care for this number "was

The nurses of Base Hospital 26 relied upon their colleagues and the values of their profession. "We talked about our days at St. Mary's with fond longing. We received more than technical training there. We observed, at close range, the meaning of self-sacrificing service. It was this, even more than what we learned, which... stuck with us through the hideous experiences in France."

quite a problem...some wards of 118 patients would have to be looked after by two day nurses and one night nurse..."[66]

In addition to surgeries, wound treatments took much of the ward nurses' time. In 1917, a French surgeon, Alexis Carrel, M.D., and an English chemist, Henry Drysdale Dakin, Ph.D., recommended the "application at frequent intervals of a gentle stream [of a weak bleach solution to treat] the whole surface of an infected wound."[67] Following these instructions, Base Hospital 26 nurses and physicians used Dakin's solution almost entirely to care for the severely infected.[68] The procedure took time and required constant monitoring. As one nurse described it "several drains are inserted [into each wound]...and into these every two hours is pumped a dark liquid, 'Dakin,'—the idea being...to keep the wound in a constant bath of antiseptic."[69]

In their spare time, the nurses reminisced about their days in Rochester:

Always our talk turned to our common tie— our training at St. Mary's. We talked about the old, familiar, daily routine, We talked about dignified Dr. Will Mayo and Dr. Charles— always with his cap at a jaunty angle; Dr. Judd, Dr. Belford and Dr. Beckman, all checking in at the hospital at 6:30 a.m...We talked about our days at St. Mary's with fond longing. We received more than technical training there. We observed, at close range, the meaning of self-sacrificing service. It was this, even more than what we learned, which...stuck with us through the hideous experiences in France.[70]

Influenza, 1918

In addition to providing trauma care, nurses at the Front had to manage an epidemic of a virulent strain of influenza. In the fall of 1918, "Spanish flu" devastated armies all over Europe.[71] The 1918 strain of influenza virus was extremely contagious and, too often, deadly. When it was accompanied by pneumonia (today recognized as acute respiratory distress syndrome), mortality was as high as 70 percent. The flu was particularly lethal for young men between the ages of 20 and 40 years, and thousands of previously healthy soldiers, crowded into cold and muddy trenches along the front lines, were especially susceptible.[72] Those who fell ill were quickly transported behind the lines to the base hospitals. By December 1918, Base Hospital 26 had received 112 patients with influenza. Nearly half of those died.[73]

Skilled nursing care was the key to the survival of those who lived. In 1918, there was no flu vaccine to prevent the disease, nor were there any antiviral medications or antibiotics with which to treat

COMMUNICATORS

"During the influenza epidemic, communication with families was a critical part of the nurses' role. At St. Mary's Hospital, "anxious relatives and friends were phoning almost incessantly," adding to the responsibilities and burdens of the nurses in charge.

the disease or its complications. Treatment consisted of giving the patients soup and tea, and bathing them to bring down fever. Vick's VapoRub, aspirin, whiskey, and cough medicine were also prescribed. For the worst cases, following doctors' orders, nurses administered morphine and oxygen to ease breathing, and digitalis to improve heart function.[74] Isolating patients in separate wards and using curtains around each bed were the two methods of controlling the spread of infection.

"...Special respiratory and pneumonia wards in which patients were masked and cubicled and the personnel masked [sic] probably did a great deal toward lessening the spread of the infection..."[75]

In the United States, civilian physicians and nurses also tried to cope with the epidemic. The deadly strain of flu, which had erupted in a Kansas military camp in the spring of 1918, swept across the country that summer. It hit Boston in late August, then Philadelphia, New York, Baltimore, Washington, and Chicago in rapid succession. Within days of the outbreak, hospitals in each of these cities were filled

Base Hospital 26 served soldiers who were ill as well as injured. Staff members set up this isolation ward to limit the spread of influenza, a global menace at the end of World War I.

to capacity, 20-bed wards stretched to accommodate 40 to 50 patients.[76] As one student nurse in New York recounted, "...Almost overnight the hospital was inundated...Wards were emptied hastily of patients convalescing from other ailments...only emergency operations were performed. Cots appeared down the center of wards...Victims came on stretchers...their faces and nails as blue as huckleberries."[77]

Following troop movement on railroad lines across the country, the flu erupted in southern Minnesota in September 1918. By this time, the Kahler Corporation was operating three hospitals in Rochester: the Colonial, the Worrall, and the Stanley. Combined with the expanded St. Mary's Hospital, beds should have been plentiful. However, this novel strain of flu was highly contagious and those with the illness could not be admitted to general surgical wards. Fortunately, Mayo physicians had an alternative. Only months before, in June 1918, the old Lincoln Hotel had been remodeled and opened as the 40-bed Isolation Hospital, under the supervision of Sister Borromeo Lenz, R.N., and Sister Dorothy Morgenthuler, R.N. On June 14, doctors had admitted the first patient, a young soldier from Fort Riley, Kansas.[78] With the full onset of the disease in the fall, Mayo Clinic physicians and nurses turned to the Isolation Hospital for additional beds.

On the Home Front, the Franciscan Sisters presciently remodeled the Lincoln Hotel into a 40-bed isolation hospital in June 1918, shortly before the outbreak of the influenza pandemic that autumn.

On October 1, 1918, Mayo physicians admitted the first two flu cases to the Isolation Hospital. The next day, they admitted a third. All three cases were mild and the patients were discharged within a few days. However, the crisis was only beginning. On October 2, patients began to arrive from other hospitals and boarding houses throughout Rochester. Within a week, the Isolation Hospital had reached its capacity. Cots were then set up wherever space permitted and patients were dismissed as soon as possible to make room for those in greater need.[79] Then, on October 7, the epidemic exploded in St. Mary's Hospital and twenty patients, eighteen of whom were nurses, had to be transferred to the Isolation Hospital.[80] According to one account, "The Sisters in charge were in great straits. The weather had been mild and the furnace had not been used since the previous spring; the house was unprovisioned for so sudden an increase of patients..."[81]

Teamwork was essential. St. Mary's Hospital was so short of nurses and general help that everyone felt it was her duty to assist, as much as possible, wherever the need was greatest.[82] Superintendent of Nurses Mary Ledwidge, R.N., was sometimes seen working in the laundry where help was utterly depleted.[83] Sisters Borromeo and Dorothy also assisted—setting up cots, cooking, and nursing patients themselves—stopping only for a few hours of sleep each night.[84]

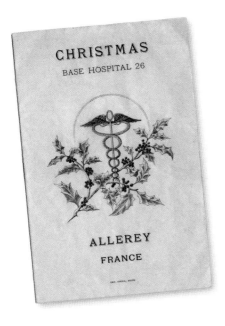

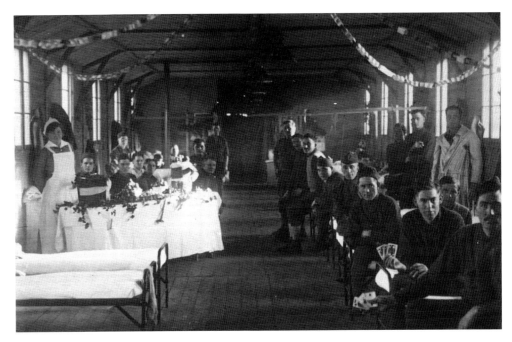

Barely a month after Armistice Day, Christmas of 1918 brought hope to the staff and patients of Base Hospital 26. Nurses helped make it a festive occasion.

Communicators

During the influenza epidemic, communication with families was a critical part of the nurses' role. At St. Mary's Hospital, "anxious relatives and friends were phoning almost incessantly," adding to the responsibilities and burdens of the nurses in charge.[85]

By December, 197 patients had been admitted to the Isolation Hospital. Twenty of those patients, including Sister Agatha O'Brien, R.N., died.

Both World War I and the influenza epidemic ended in the late fall of 1918. Armistice was declared on November 11, while the flu subsided gradually that month, tapering off even more in December. A week after the armistice, Ida Anderson, R.N., wrote home from the Front, noting:

"...When the Christmas bells peal forth 'Peace on earth'...may we all endeavor to make it a lasting peace...I cannot describe the feeling of knowing that victory has blessed the Allies and this terrible slaughter is at an end."[86]

Soon thereafter, the Christmas spirit got hold of everybody and plans for a Christmas away from home on the Front began to materialize and for the most part worked out by the nurses.[87]

The holiday season brought joy to those in Rochester as well. The influenza epidemic was subsiding and with the armistice, friends, colleagues, and family members would soon return from the war. Miriam Johnson, R.N., recalled:

I'll never forget Armistice Day. I was on duty on second floor Colonial on November 11, 1918, at 11:00 A.M. All the bells in Rochester started ringing, signaling the end of World War I. It was a joyful time, with nurses and doctors crying and laughing as we embraced each other.[88]

45

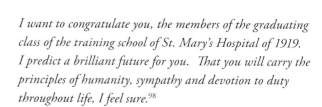

Seven weeks later, the New Year would bring a resurgence of influenza, interrupting Rochester's celebratory mood. From January through March 1919, nurses at the Isolation Hospital admitted 131 more patients suffering with influenza complicated with pneumonia. By May 1919, when the epidemic finally subsided, a total of 360 patients had been hospitalized in Rochester and 41 had died. Those who lived owed their lives to the compassionate nursing care they had received from the devoted Sisters and the student nurses who worked around the clock for months.

That spring, in his commencement speech to the Class of 1919, Dr. Will expressed his confidence in the graduating students:

I want to congratulate you, the members of the graduating class of the training school of St. Mary's Hospital of 1919. I predict a brilliant future for you. That you will carry the principles of humanity, sympathy and devotion to duty throughout life, I feel sure.[98]

Kahler School of Nursing

The next year, Dr. Will could have said the same to members of the first graduating class of the new nursing school in Rochester. In 1920, ten students completed the original two-year program launched during the war by the Colonial Hospital Training School for Nurses. They, too, had been educated in an atmosphere that focused on humanity, sympathy, and devotion to duty.[90] During their training, the school changed its name to the Colonial and Allied Hospitals' School of Nurses. In 1921, the name changed again to Kahler Hospital's School of Nursing. Professional pride was evident in the description of the school's iconic pin:

The Kahler pin is composed of a cross, caduceus, and Florence Nightingale lamp...the cross is a combination of the Pattee and Maltese crosses—symbolizing those

Above: *The Kahler nurses' pin featured the lamp of Florence Nightingale and other symbolic elements.* ***Left:*** *The classical-style portico of the Colonial Hospital formed a backdrop for this early photo of Kahler nurses.*

who shield and care for the weak...The caduceus represents power, wisdom, diligence and activity...and the Nightingale lamp symbolizes good deeds shining through darkness.[91]

It was now a three-year program with Bertha Johnson, R.N., serving as director.[92] That year, Dr. Charlie was inadvertently caught up in the nursing profession's debate over the educational preparation of professional nurses when he recommended training 100,000 country girls as sub-nurses to help address the nursing shortage. His opinion, widely publicized in the *Pictorial Review,* caused quite a reaction from

Irene English, R.N., was recruited to lead the Kahler Hospital's School of Nursing in 1923. She was a transformational leader in establishing the school's national reputation for excellence in nursing education.

nursing leaders who were already embroiled in a debate standardizing nursing educational requirements. In fact, Dr. Charlie's opinion was in direct contrast to the results of a national study on nursing education commissioned by the Rockefeller Foundation and published in the *Goldmark Report.* Shaped by the views of nurse educators at Teachers College and the 1910 *Flexner Report* on medical education, the *Goldmark Report* supported nursing leaders' demands for improvements in the educational process for nurses and advocated fully funded training schools and a graded curriculum of 28 months.[93]

Despite the controversy, nurses in Rochester did not have to worry; the Kahler School of Nursing, with its three-year course of study, was already well within the new national guidelines and had been accredited by the Minnesota Board of Nursing in 1920. The school's reputation would continue to rise, when Irene English, R.N., president of the State Registered Nurses Association, became its director in 1923. Under her leadership, the school grew in size and prestige, placing among the top ten nursing schools in the United States.[94] A sense of purpose and pride inspired the students. In an article called "First Impressions," one alumna wrote, "Our uniforms...rustled crisply as we stepped on the elevator which was to convey us to our newly assigned duty."[95]

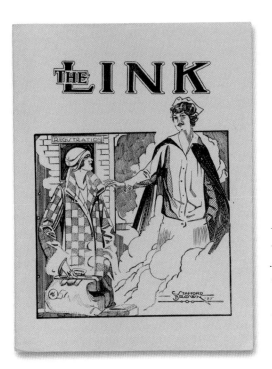

Alumnae publications Alumnae Quarterly, *from Saint Marys school, and* The Link *(pictured), from the Kahler school, kept them connected to their roots.*

The Kahler Student Experience

In some ways, The Kahler School of Nursing student experience was typical of that of many diploma schools in the 1920s.

Miriam Johnson, R.N., recalled three years of rigorous training at the Colonial, Worrall, and other downtown hospitals owned by the Kahler Corporation.[96] There, nurse supervisors assisted instructors as they taught students the basics of nursing. "Back then, basic patient care was called Nursing Arts...it included giving patients daily baths, taking a patient outdoors in a wheelchair for some fresh air and giving lots of backrubs."[97] Along with 519 hours of classes such as the Principles and Practice of Nursing, Drugs and Solutions, Bacteriology, Ethics, Hospital Economics, Bandaging, and *Materia Medica,* pupil nurses

Kahler nursing students enjoyed the hospitality of Dr. Will's riverboat, the North Star.

(as they were called then) learned by watching their instructors.[98] Shifts were 7:30 a.m. to 7:30 p.m. or a split shift of 7:30 a.m. to 1:00 p.m. and 5:00 to 7:30 p.m.; night shifts were 7:30 p.m. to 7:30 a.m., with two hours off for rest if the workload allowed.

On Sunday afternoons, students occasionally had a few hours of rest. Other times, they might make rounds with Dr. Will or Dr. Charlie, who often stopped by the wards to review patient charts and make sure everyone was getting the best possible care.[99]

Both inside and outside of the hospital, Kahler students obeyed strict rules, rigid schedules (lights out at 10:00 p.m.), requisite study hours, and were allowed only one late pass each month.[100] Nonetheless, they also found time for fun, participating in the glee club and orchestra, taking swim lessons, attending concerts in the civic auditorium, and joining in winter sleigh rides. Indeed, the "Kahlerites," as they often called themselves, had fond memories of teas, banquets, and other festivities including picnics at Silver Lake and Mayowood,

Saint Marys Training School nurses studied in the library, circa 1924.

the country estate of Dr. Charlie and his wife, Edith, as well as excursions on the Mississippi River.

One student recalled a trip on Dr. Will's riverboat, the *NorthStar*:

'Dame Nature' smiled kindly on the morning of May 26th and bestowed upon the seniors a beautiful and enchanting day for their boat trip given by Dr. and Mrs. W. J. Mayo and Mr. and Mrs. John Kahler...We boarded the vessel about ten o'clock—soon Captain Rickman was piloting us up river...at twelve o'clock we approached a village called Alma... Here we stopped to eat lunch on the shore... About three o'clock we began to retrace our course, and five o'clock found us drawing into port at Wabasha...That evening a tired and sunburned group of girls entered Rochester...[101]

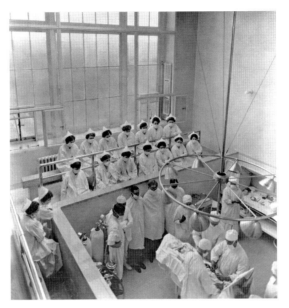

Student nurses observed surgery at St. Mary's Hospital, circa 1924.

"Mayo Methods"

For both St. Mary's and Kahler graduates, the Mayo Clinic reputation preceded the nurses everywhere they went. As one patient put it, the new graduates were "encircled with the halo of Mayo prestige."[102] Mary Ledwidge, R.N., superintendent of nurses at St. Mary's Hospital from 1914 to 1920, agreed:

Just as surgeons who have been associated with the Mayo brothers are accepted as being at the top of their profession, nurses who have received their training in the Mayo hospital secure the best positions at their graduation... Hospital authorities want Mayo nurses because they want Mayo methods.[103]

Those who hired Rochester nurses most certainly got Mayo methods. Mary Ledwidge noted the fact in an interview for a Little Rock, Arkansas, newspaper, stating that she could "walk into any operating room in America [and] tell at a glance" if it was under the charge of a graduate from a Mayo hospital."[104] The nurse would have the operating room arranged just as the Mayo brothers had theirs situated. "She would be lost in an operating room arranged differently..."[105]

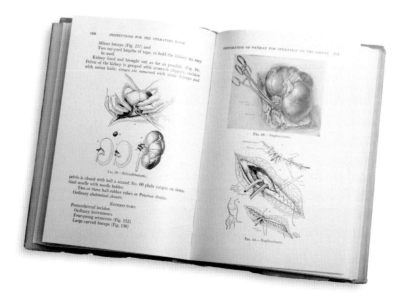

A page from the book, The Operating Room: Instructions for Nurses and Assistants *was first published in 1920 by St. Mary's Hospital. With five subsequent editions, it was used for many years across the world to teach.*

49

Visionary Leadership

By the early 1920s, the hospitals affiliated with Mayo Clinic were again outgrowing their bed capacity. In particular, the growing number of surgeries being done in Rochester dictated the need for additional surgical beds, and on May 12, 1922, a new surgical pavilion opened at St. Mary's Hospital, beginning a new phase of the hospital.[106] The addition, almost singlehandedly planned by Sister Joseph, had modern operating rooms, pathology laboratories, and rooms for surgical patients surpassing anything in the past.[107] Beginning at ten in the morning when the doors were opened to the public, the crowds continued in a constant stream until six in the evening while an orchestra in the small sun parlor played throughout the day.[108]

Mayo Clinic opened a new diagnostic building in 1928, later named for its principal designer, Henry Plummer, M.D.

During the opening ceremonies, Henry Plummer, M.D., lauded Sister Joseph's visionary leadership:

The genius, faith and vision of Sister Joseph put this big thing through. Only someone of great genius and great faith would dare to double the size of this already great hospital...She had the vision and the greatness to do it.[109]

Dr. Will also praised Sister Joseph for her role in planning the new pavilion and in the development of St. Mary's Hospital over time, noting that she had served in almost every capacity in the work of the hospital.[110] In his remarks, Dr. Will commented on Sister Joseph's leadership qualities, stating:

Executives of the character of Sister Mary Joseph are born, not made. Of tireless industry, strong individualism and personality, with intellectual capacity of the highest order...she has been the guiding spirit and presiding genius of St. Mary's Hospital.[111]

In this kitchen at St. Mary's Hospital, nurses prepared nutritious and diet-specific meal trays for delivery to patient rooms. The Franciscan Sisters owned a nearby farm, which provided fresh food for patients.

Sister Joseph's response to the praise was modest, befitting her personality, "I have worked for many years to make St. Mary's hospital a house of God and a gateway to heaven for His many suffering children."[112]

The expansion of St. Mary's Hospital reflected the growing trend of specialization in nursing, which paralleled the rise in medical specialization in the first half of the twentieth century. With an entire pavilion dedicated to the care of surgical patients, other areas of St. Mary's Hospital and other areas of the downtown hospitals could be dedicated to various clinical specialties. St. Mary's would now devote specific units to pediatrics, medical, and obstetrical patients; Colonial was designated for urology, orthopedics, and general surgery; Worrall focused on conditions of the eye, ear, nose and throat; and Curie specialized in radiology. Meanwhile, Mayo Clinic continued to add its own new buildings.

Photo credit: Associated Press

Sister Joseph Dempsey, superintendent of St. Mary's Hospital, greeted President Franklin Roosevelt when he came to Rochester in 1934 to honor the Mayo brothers on behalf of the American Legion.

A National Reputation

In 1934, national attention turned to Rochester. President Franklin Roosevelt presented a citation for distinguished service to the Mayo brothers on behalf of the American Legion. Following his address, President Roosevelt visited St. Mary's Hospital, where he paid tribute to the Sisters. The moment, captured by newspaper reporters, reflected the growing reputation of nursing in Rochester, Minnesota.

That reputation would continue to grow. During the 1930s, nurses at St. Mary's Hospital and the hospitals of the Kahler Corporation continued to have unparalleled access to the thinking of famous physicians and nurses through the Mayo doctors' connections. In addition, the Mayo brothers themselves continued to be involved with the education of student nurses, interacting with them in the classroom and on the wards. As Marian Hall, R.N., Kahler School of Nursing graduate recalled, "Dr. Charlie and Dr. Will, they'd go around together. Dr. Charlie would sit on the bed and talk to patients; Dr. Will was pretty straight. He didn't do that."[113] Sister Antoine Murphy, R.N., who began nursing in Rochester in 1938, recalled being in bacteriology lab as a student nurse when "there was a knock on the door...It was Dr. Will and Dr. Charlie and they walked around and talked with the students..."[114]

Transformational Leadership

St. Mary's and Kahler nurse leaders had unprecedented autonomy over nursing practice and nursing education. For example, in order to staff two wings of the Joseph Building in 1936, Sister Ancina Adams recommended to Sister Domitilla DuRocher that St. Mary's employ graduate nurses rather than student nurses, as had been the tradition. It was the middle of the Great Depression and St. Mary's had decreased its school's enrollment because patient census was down by forty percent and opportunities for the school's graduates to find private duty jobs after graduation were limited. Without further discussion—or apparently any consultation with physicians—Sister Domitilla advised Sister Ancina to "go with God" in making her decision.[115] The next day the new staffing model was adopted.

The same autonomy in decision making held for nursing education. As early as 1923, Sister Domitilla had added postgraduate training in surgical nursing and operating room technique for registered nurses. In 1936, she agreed that St. Mary's Hospital School of Nursing (the name adopted in 1932) should cooperate with the College of Saint Teresa in Winona, Minnesota, providing clinical experience for their five-year bachelor of science in nursing (B.S.N.) program.[116]

In 1937, not only did St. Mary's begin to admit men to their program, its leaders also appointed Ruth Hugelen, R.N., as the school's first full-time supervisor of clinical instruction. Meanwhile, at the Kahler School of Nursing, Superintendent Irene English, R.N., and later, Lulu Saunders, R.N., focused increasing attention on the educational needs of students, rather than seeing them solely as a source of staffing for the hospital.[117] In that light, in 1939, Kahler School of Nursing leaders established a new position, appointing Marian Zulley, R.N., to serve as Supervisor of Clinical Instruction.

Following the death of Sister Joseph Dempsey in 1939, Sister Domitilla DuRocher, R.N., assumed the leadership of St. Mary's Hospital.

An Era Ends

The year 1939 brought the end of an era, as death claimed four of the men and women who had played decisive roles in the development of Mayo Clinic and St. Mary's Hospital.[118]

On March 29, Sister Joseph died peacefully at St. Mary's Hospital after serving there for 47 years. She was eulogized by many for her life's work. Dr. Will took the lead, reflecting, "As my brother and I look back over the years of her devoted service, we can only say that Sister Mary Joseph has done more for the welfare of the sick than any other woman whom we know. She will be held in honored memory."[119] Sister Joseph's combination of leadership and teamwork inspired this reflection:

The phenomenal growth of the hospital was due in large measure to the genius of the Doctors Mayo...It was due in equal measure to the leadership of Sister Joseph and the tireless work and cooperation she and her Sisters put into the hospital.[120]

On May 26, Dr. Charlie died of pneumonia, and the Rochester nurses filed by his casket to pay respects to a beloved colleague, friend, and mentor. His death was followed on July 5 by that of Anna Jamme, the first superintendent of St. Mary's School of Nursing. Then on July 28, Dr. Will died peacefully in his sleep. The deaths of these leaders, in such close succession, saddened the Rochester community. The Mayo Clinic Surgical Society wrote this reaction to the Mayo brothers' deaths in a resolution recorded in the Society's minutes, noting:

Nurses formed a line of honor to pay respects to Dr. Charlie as his funeral procession passed through downtown Rochester.

Those who in years to come peruse these minutes may justly question what manner of men were we, who in experiencing bereavement such as ours in recent months, yet inadequately expressed it. Let them remember then, that those whose greatness they strive to recreate...were living men with whom we walked and talked and laughed; our preceptors, our colleagues, our friends. We are too close to this grief to describe it: 'True sorrow makes a silence in the heart.'[121]

The Mayo brothers died within two months of each other in 1939, shortly before the outbreak of World War II in Europe. By planning carefully and graciously welcoming younger colleagues to positions of leadership, they ensured that Mayo Clinic would continue to thrive after their lifetimes.

The nurses' grief was recorded in their actions rather than in their words. As the funeral cortége passed St. Mary's and Colonial hospitals, hundreds of nurses lined the streets to pay their respects.

Despite the loss of its founders, the Mayos' legacy would continue. Indeed, one of the strengths of Mayo Clinic, even at this early stage, was succession planning for an orderly and effective transition of leadership. The Mayo brothers had retired from surgery in the late 1920s and from active administration in the early 1930s, and new leaders were already in place. So, while the Mayo brothers' deaths marked the end of an era, the Clinic would not only survive, but grow. On September 30, 1939, the 50th anniversary of the opening of St. Mary's

Hospital, the Franciscan Sisters broke ground for a 375-bed addition that would expand the facility to 850 beds. Following Sister Joseph, Sister Domitilla DuRocher assumed the role of hospital administrator.[122] Together with the director of nursing at Kahler Hospital, and in collaboration with Mayo Clinic colleagues, a new team would face a rapidly changing future—one in which wars, epidemics, scientific medicine, and new technology would figure prominently.

ENDNOTES

1. Amy Hahn, "Heritage of Caring: Saint Marys School of Nursing Celebrates 100 Years of Caregiving," *Rochester Women* (September/October 2006): 68. Mayo Historical Unit, Saint Marys School of Nursing File.

2. Ibid., 67-68.

3. "Improved X-Ray Methods Developed at Mayo Clinic," *Science Newsletter,* 19, 517 (March 7, 1931): 148. See also Anita Reimer, "Nasal Catheter Suction," *The Link* (1930): 1-2. Mayo Historical Unit; and Esther Athen, "The Oxygen Chamber," *The Link* (June 1926): 55. Mayo Historical Unit. See also John Graner, *A History of the Department of Internal Medicine at the Mayo Clinic* (Rochester: Mayo Foundation for Medical Education and Research, 2002): 6-7, 22. Drs. Banting, Best, and Macleod visited Mayo Clinic in the autumn of 1922 to present their results on the discovery of insulin.

4. Virginia Wentzel, "Elsie Evelyn Krug": 1. Reprint: Rochester. Mayo Historical Unit, Saint Marys School of Nursing archives.

5. Jane Champion, interview as referenced in Whelan, *Sisters Story,* 115 (see Prologue, n. 12).

6. *Nursing Historical Highlights* (Rochester: Mayo Foundation for Medical Education and Research, 2012).

7. Virginia S. Wentzel, *Sincere et Constanter, 1906-1970: The Story of Saint Marys School of Nursing* (Rochester: Mayo Foundation for Medical Education and Research, 2006): 34.

8. Ibid.; see also school catalogues, *St. Mary's Hospital Training School,* and *St. Mary's Hospital Annual Reports,* 1920s and 1930s.

9. Elsie Krug, T*he Pattern Changes,* (1990): 19.

10. Sister Antonia Rostomily, "Untitled" (unpublished paper, St. Mary's School of Nursing archives, Mayo Clinic, Rochester, MN, 1939).

11. Harry M. Harwick, *Forty-four Years with the Mayo Clinic: 1908-1952* (Rochester: Whiting Press): 10.

12. William Holmes, *Dedicated to Excellence:* The Rochester Methodist Hospital Story (Rochester: Johnson Printing Co., 1987): 41.

13. Ibid.

14. *History of Saint Marys,* 1. Saint Marys School of Nursing; see also May MacGregor Givens and Lillian MacGregor Shaw, *Please Nurse: Memoirs of May MacGregor Given's Life as a Nurse with the American Army in France, in 1918,* 4.

15. "The Origins and Development of Saint Marys," *St. Mary's School of Nursing (SMSN) Annual Report, 1920:* 2. Mayo Historical Unit.

16. Sylvia Rinker, "To Cultivate a Feeling of Confidence: The Nursing of Obstetric Patients, 1890-1940," *Nursing History Review,* 8 (2000): 117-142.

17. "Pediatrics and the History of the Mayo Foundation": 1-7. Reprint: Rochester. Mayo Historical Unit.

18. Mayo Clinic, "The Growth of the Early Clinic," www.mayoclinic.org/tradition-heritage/1914-building.html (accessed July 14, 2012; site now discontinued).

19. Ibid.

20. Helen Clapesattle, *The Doctors Mayo* (Minneapolis: University of Minnesota Press, 1941): 323.

21. Ibid.

22. Graner, *History of the Department of Internal Medicine,* 4.

23. Clapesattle, *Doctors Mayo,* 326.

24. Ibid.

25. Clark Nelson, *Mayo Roots: Profiling the Origins of Mayo Clinic* (Rochester: Mayo Foundation for Medical Education and Research, 1990): 260.

26. Mark Davis, *Mayo Clinic Dermatology: The First Ninety Years* (Rochester: Mayo Foundation for Medical Education and Research, 2007).

27. Arlene Crepps, "The Art of Dermatologic Nursing," *The Link* (November 1939).

28. Ibid.

29. Ibid.

30. Susan Reverby, *Ordered to Care: The Dilemma of American Nursing,* 1850-1945 (Cambridge: Cambridge University Press, 1987).

31. Martha Schuman, "Alumnae News," *Quarterly Report of the Alumnae Association of St. Mary's* (April 1916).

32. Reverby, *Ordered to Care.*

33. Arlene Keeling, "Alert to the Necessities of the Emergency: U.S. Nursing During the 1918 Influenza Pandemic," *Public Health Reports: Special Supplement on Pandemic Influenza,* 125, 3 (April, 2010): 105-113. See also Arlene Keeling, "When the City is a Great Field Hospital: The Influenza Pandemic and the New York City Nursing Response," *The Journal of Clinical Nursing,* 18 (September 2009): 2732-2738; and Public Health Reports, Supplement, 125, 3 (April 2010): 3-134.

34. See "Chapter VII," *Sketch of the History of the Mayo Clinic and Mayo Foundation* (Philadelphia: WB Saunders, Co, 1926): 92-99. Reprint, Mayo Historical Unit.

35. *History of Base Hospital 26, December 15th, 1917 to May 3rd, 1919* (Minneapolis: D.D.

Getchell, 1920). Mayo Historical Unit.

36 Arlene Keeling, "Chapter 2: Nurse Anesthetists, 1900-1938," *Nursing and the Privilege of Prescription* (Columbus: Ohio State University Press, 2007): 40.

37 The Red Cross," *Military Surgeon,* 39, 2 (August 1916): 202.

38 "Alumnae News," *Quarterly Report of the St. Marys Hospital Training School,* 1, 1 (April 1916). Mayo Historical Unit, Saint Marys School of Nursing archives. As reported in the St. Mary's "Alumnae News" in April of 1916, "Since the prospect of this country's becoming embroiled in the world war arose, a number of the Alumnae members applied for enrollment in the Red Cross Service and have been accepted."

39 Lawrence Gooley, "Florence Bullard: Local Nurse, World War One Hero," www.adirondeckalmanac.com/2011/06/florence-bullard-local-nurse-world-war.html (site now discontinued).

40 Frances Bullard, "Letter written September 26, 1917," St. Mary's Alumnae Quarterly (November, 1917).

41 Gooley, "Florence Bullard: Local Nurse, World War One Hero." See also Christine Hallet, *Containing Trauma: Nursing Work in the First World War* (Manchester: Manchester University Press, 2005).

42 Gooley, "Florence Bullard: Local Nurse, World War One Hero."

43 Hallet, *Containing Trauma,* 107.

44 Mary Hines, Mayo Historical Unit, People File, MHU-0675.

45 Ibid.

46 Sister Mary Bertilla Lebens, "Memoirs of Sister Bertilla in the Operating Room with Dr. Charlie and Dr. Will Mayo, 1917 -1940" (transcript of interview): 1. Saint Marys archives.

47 Ibid., 949.

48 Mary T. Sarnecky, *A History of the U.S. Army Nurse Corps* (Philadelphia: University of Pennsylvania Press, 1999): 130.

49 Ibid., 131.

50 *History of Base Hospital 26, December 15th, 1917 to May 3rd, 1919.* Mayo Historical Unit. The nurses sailed on the Baltic, while the enlisted men sailed on the *Adriatic.* Both ships were in the same convoy across the Atlantic.

51 "Hospital Center in France," *Saint Marys School of Nursing, 1919 Annual Report:* 1-2. Reprint: Rochester. Mayo Historical Unit.

52 MacGregor Given, *Please Nurse,* 5-6.

53 Ibid., 6.

54 Ibid.

55 Col. Donald Macrae (Medical Corps Commanding), *History of Hospital Unit 'K,' U.S. Army and Mobile Hospital #1,* AEF (Council Bluffs, Iowa: 1938): 20-21. Office of Medical History, AMEDD Center of History and Heritage Office Files WWI, Box 40 D, Fort Sam Houston, Texas.

56 MacGregor Given, *Please Nurse,* 8.

57 Lorrie A. Bennett and Barbara A. Jerabek, "Sophie Gran Jevene Winton: A Woman and Nurse Anesthetist. Before Her Time: April 24, 1887- April 24, 1989" (master's thesis, Mayo School of Health Related Sciences, Rochester, Minnesota, 1999). Archives of the AANA.

58 Winifred Ashba, correspondence, *The Link,* September 1919.

59 Nell Bryant, correspondence, July 23, 1918. Mayo Historical Unit.

60 Carolyn S. Beck, "Historical Profiles of Mayo: A Mayo Nurses' Moment in World War I France," *Mayo Clinic Proceedings,* 74 (1999): 1060. Reprint: Rochester. Mayo Historical Unit.

61 *Base Hospital #26, A History* (1918):6. Mayo Historical Unit.

62 Ibid., 53.

63 Oliver Beahrs (1995): 198.

64 *Base Hospital #26,* 18.

65 May MacGregor Given, correspondence, September 23, 1923, quote p. 11.

66 *Base Hospital #26,* 34.

67 Army Medical Services, "Carrel-Dakin Treatment of Wounds," *The British Medical Journal, 2, 2966* (November 3, 1917): 597.

68 *Base Hospital #26,* 26.

69 "Mademoiselle Miss: Letters from an American Girl Serving with the Rank of Lieutenant in a French Army Hospital at the Front" (Boston: WA Butterfield, 1916) in Arlene Keeling, "Historical Research and WOC Nursing: A Strange and Wonderful Relationship," *Journal of Wound, Ostomy and Continence Nursing,* 29 (2002): 180-183 quote p. 181.

70 MacGregor Given, *Please Nurse.* The reference was to Dr. Balfour.

71 Carol Byerly, *Fever of War: The Influenza Epidemic in the U.S. Army During World War I* (New York: The New York University Press, 2005).

72 Ibid.

73 *Base Hospital #26,* 26.

74 Arlene Keeling, "Alert to the Necessities of the Emergency," *Public Health Reports, Special Supplement on Pandemic Influenza,* 3, 125 Supplement (April 2010): 105-112.

75 *Base Hospital #26.*

76 Keeling, "Alert to the Necessities," 108.

77 D. Deming, "Influenza, 1918: Reliving the Great Epidemic," *American Journal of Nursing,* 10 (1957): 1308-9. See also Keeling, "Alert to the Necessities," 109.

78 *St. Mary's Hospital Annals* (1918):109. Mayo Historical Unit, Folder Influenza.

79 Ibid., 110.

80 Ibid., 110.

81 Ibid.

82 Ibid., 111.

83 Ibid.

84 Sister Ellen Whelan, *The Sisters' Story: Saint Marys Hospital-Mayo Clinic, 1889 to 1939* (Rochester: Mayo Foundation for Medical Education and Research, 2002): 105.

85 Ibid., 110-111.

86 *The Echo,* 3, 4 (November 1918). Saint Marys School of Nursing archives.

87 *Base Hospital #26,* 55.

88 Kelly Erickson, "Kahler School of Nursing Student Reminisces 65 Years After Graduation," *Chronolith* (Winter 1988): 17-20. Olmsted County Historical Society, Methodist Kahler School of Nursing.

89 William J. Mayo, "Address to the Graduates" (1919): 1-4. Mayo Historical Unit, Folder Saint Marys School of Nursing Annual Report.

90 *50 Years Serving Humanity Through Education: The Methodist Kahler School of Nursing, Rochester Minnesota,* 1918-1968, 6. MHU.

91 Evelyn Soucek, "The Kahler Pin." Mayo Historical Unit, MKSN File.

92 Sketch, 98. See also *Nursing Historical Highlights* (Rochester: Minn: Mayo Foundation for Medical Education and Research, 2012): 13.

93 Reverby, *Ordered to Care,* 164-65.

94 Roy Watson, "A History of the Kahler School of Nursing" (December 9, 1924): 1-3. Mayo Historical Unit, MKSN File.

95 Ragna Nielson, "First Impressions," *The Link* (November 1933).

96 Erickson, "Kahler School of Nursing Student," 18.

97 Ibid.

98 "Kahler School of Nursing, 1929-30 First Year Course of Study": 1. Reprint: Rochester. Mayo Historical Unit, Kahler File, MHU-0676.

99 Erickson, "Kahler School of Nursing Student,"19.

100 Ibid.

101 G. Eastman and M. Blair, "The Boat Trip," *The Link,* V, 1 (n.d.): n.p. Mayo Historical Unit.

102 Anonymous patient, "Reminiscences of Saint Marys," *Saint Marys School of Nursing Annual Report* (1919): 4.

103 "The Demand for Mayo Nurses Never has Been Supplied," *Little Rock Arkansas, Dem.* (Tuesday, November 30, 1920). Mayo Historical Unit, Saint Marys School of Nursing File.

104 Ibid.

105 Ibid.

106 Marianne L. Hockema, "The Franciscan Five Saint Marys Hospital's Sister Administrators" (presentation, 2002): 19.

107 Sister Mary Brigh, "Medical History in Minnesota: A Symposium" (paper read at the 57th Annual Meeting of the Medical Library Association, Rochester, Minnesota, June 2-6, 1958): 26 .

108 "Formal Opening of Saint Marys Surgical Pavilion, May 12, 1922," *St. Mary's Alumnae Quarterly* (1922): 3.

109 Hockema, "The Franciscan Five," 19.

110 William James Mayo, "A Tribute from William J. Mayo" (1922). Mayo Historical Unit, People File, MHU-0675.

111 Ibid.

112 Sister Mary Joseph Dempsey (1856-1939): 1-3. Mayo Historical Unit, People File, MHU-0675.

113 Jeff Hansel, "Nursing Circa 1930," *Post-Bulletin* (May 2, 2005). Reprint: Rochester. Olmsted County Historical Society, Methodist Kahler Box, D-102.

114 Ibid.

115 *Historical Overview: Common Themes:* 4-5. Reprint: Rochester. Mayo Historical Unit.

116 "For Fifty Years: Going Forth to Serve," "A Tree must Grow."Reprint: Rochester. Mayo Historical Unit.

117 *The Link,* 1, 6 (n.d.): 2. Reprint: Rochester. Mayo Historical Unit. Irene English was previously superintendent of nurses at Northern Pacific Hospital, St. Paul, and faculty at the University of Minnesota.

118 "For 50 Years, Going Forth to Serve." Reprint: Rochester. Mayo Historical Unit.

119 William J. Mayo, eulogy, 1939.

120 Sister Mary Joseph Dempsey, 1856-1939. Mayo Historical Unit, People File, MHU-0675.

121 "Minutes of the Meeting," Mayo Clinic Surgical Society (1939): 2.

122 Sister Mary Brigh, "Medical History in Minnesota: A Symposium" (paper read at the 57th Annual Meeting of the Medical Library Association, Rochester, Minnesota, June 2-6, 1958).

During World War II, Mayo Clinic nurses provided care in virtually every theater of combat as well as on the home front.

CHAPTER III

MAYO INFLUENCES, NURSING TRANSITIONS

1940-1970

Nurses who served in the Mayo Units in New Guinea during World War II were part of the post-war transformation of medicine.

Training and working at Mayo-affiliated hospitals influenced nurses in significant ways, some of which the nurses recognized only later in their lives. Recent graduates might notice the influences when they left Rochester and had to adapt to new places and practices. Nurses who remained in Rochester would tap those influences to transform their practice as new nursing care models, innovative treatments, additional technologies, and advances in medical and nursing knowledge became available.

Nurses working in Mayo-affiliated hospitals learned that they were expected to adapt to change, they were valuable members of the health care team, they should use scientific methods and modern equipment, and they should meet the patient's needs first. Mayo Clinic standards also emphasized nondiscrimination on the basis of age, race, gender, creed, and color—a principle that would become increasingly important as the twentieth century progressed.

During the period from 1940 to 1970, nurses affiliated with Mayo Clinic would understand the strength of these influences as they dealt with profound changes in the world and in the professions of medicine and nursing. At mid century, with the rise of specialization in both medicine and nursing, the increased use of complex technology in patient care and dramatic changes in the political, social, and economic context in which they worked, the nurses would have to transform their practice while maintaining core values. As the decade of the 1940s opened, no changes would be as significant as those introduced by the Second World War.

"Every nurse is giving her utmost"

Even before the United States entered World War II in 1941, some graduates of the Saint Marys and Kahler nursing schools were already serving with the Allies in Europe. Martha Thevoz, R.N., was working in the American Hospital in Paris when the Germans attacked the city in 1940. Describing that day in a letter to her colleagues back home, she captured the essence of what she had learned in Rochester— dedication to the patient as the priority of care.

...War is more or less at Paris' gates. Yesterday, June 3rd, there was heavy bombing of the city... We are at our post near our wounded soldiers during the bombardment. Our first duties on the floors are: Close the shutters and windows, draw the curtains, close the gas and stay with the patients. These men, during an air raid, get very nervous because they have just come from the battlefields where they were so heavily bombarded. Now, there are over 100 men here—mostly head or spinal cases...These men are desperately ill and have suffered such a great shock...Every nurse is giving her utmost...[1]

Meanwhile, other "Kahler Girls" (as they called themselves) as well as graduates of Saint Marys School of Nursing had already joined the U.S. Army and Navy Nurse Corps and were stationed on military bases at home or on hospital ships around the world.[2] Kahler graduate Ruth Erickson, R.N., joined the Navy Nurse Corps in 1936 and served on the U.S.S. *Relief* from November 1938 to April 1940, when she was transferred to the U.S. Naval

Hospital in Pearl Harbor, Hawaii. She was there, talking over coffee, on December 7, 1941, when the first Japanese planes attacked. Recalling the day that was supposed to have been her Sunday off, she said:

Ruth Erickson, R.N., alumna of the Kahler nursing school, served with the Navy Nurse Corps in Hawaii and helped care for wounded survivors when the Japanese attacked Pearl Harbor on Dec. 7, 1941: "We gave those gravely injured patients sedatives for their intense pain."

My heart was racing, the telephone was ringing, the chief nurse...saying, 'Girls, get into your uniforms at once! This is the real thing!'...I was in my room by that time; changing into uniform...Smoke was rising from the burning ships...I ran to the orthopedic dressing room... drew water into every container...and set up the instrument boiler...The first patient came at 8:25 a.m. with a large opening in his abdomen and bleeding profusely...Then the burned patients streamed in...There was heavy oil on the water and the men had dived off the ship and swum through it to Hospital Point...We gave those gravely injured patients sedatives for their intense pain ...[3]

Working all day and night for more than a week along with military physicians and other nurses on duty in Pearl Harbor, Ruth Erickson cared for hundreds of critically injured sailors, trying desperately to save as many as she could. Ten days later, ordered to temporary duty on the S.S. *President Coolidge*, she accompanied the patients who were being evacuated to the mainland for further treatment.[4] For Ruth Erickson, who would attain the rank of captain and be appointed to a four-year term as director of the United States Navy Nurse Corps, patients always came first.

With America's declaration of war, the military mobilized teams of medical and nursing personnel for deployment—some to Europe and others to the Pacific. Among these was the Mayo Unit, organized in 1941 as the 71st General Hospital by Charles W. Mayo, M.D. (Dr. Chuck), son of Dr. Charlie and grandson of Dr. William Worrall Mayo.[5] The 71st General Hospital was officered almost entirely by Mayo Clinic staff physicians and fellows and included many nurses who had trained at Mayo-affiliated hospitals.[6]

By 1942, Rochester was the site of numerous celebrations and farewell parties as one after another, nurses and physicians said goodbye to their colleagues and headed for training camps throughout the United States. One party held on the afternoon of September 17, 1942 was described:

The Kahler Alumnae Association gave a tea at the Damon Hotel, having as their honored guests the Kahler Alumnae affiliated with Base Hospital Unit 71 of the Mayo Clinic. At this time a service flag was presented and dedicated to all Kahler Alumnae who are serving with the Armed Forces.[7]

After months of meetings and drills in Rochester, the nurses of the 71st General Army Hospital left for South Carolina in December 1942. The fledgling army nurses were bound for Stark General Army Hospital to join the 89th General Hospital for basic training. It would

Drs. James Priestley (left) and Charles W. (Chuck) Mayo commanded the two Mayo-sponsored Army hospital units in the Pacific Theater of World War II.

be the first of several assignments before they departed the United States for duty in the Pacific.[8]

While the young graduates were involved with military life in South Carolina—drilling with gas masks, swinging across moats on ropes, hiking in the moonlight, and eating hamburgers at the Officers' Club, back in Rochester, the two nursing schools associated with Mayo Clinic were doing their part to train new nurses.[9] The demand for professional nurses was great. The nursing shortage in the United States was already severe and becoming worse as increasing numbers of nurses left for the war. To the military and public health leaders in charge, the solution was simple: nursing schools should produce more graduates at a faster pace.

Cadet Nurse Corps

On March 29, 1943, Ohio Congresswoman Frances Payne Bolton, introduced legislation proposing the establishment of a government program to fund nursing education for students who promised to remain in nursing for the duration of World War II.[10] Only three months later, on July 1, 1943, the 78th Congress passed the Nurse Training Act (also known as the Bolton Act) into law.[11] It encompassed the Cadet Nurse Corps Program, an initiative that provided funding for nursing schools throughout the United States to assure a supply of nurses for the armed forces, governmental and civilian hospitals, and health agencies for the duration of the war.[12] Students who entered the Cadet Nurse Corps under the Bolton Act had their tuition, fees, and books paid for and were given uniforms with the appropriate insignia and a monthly stipend.[13] The program of study was shortened to thirty months rather than thirty-six, and student nursing care could be provided in hospitals or other settings even as they were in their senior year.[14]

Both Saint Marys School of Nursing and the Kahler School of Nursing participated in the national program. Lulu Saunders, R.N., Kahler's educational director, explained plans for the seniors' final months of training:

...Services which have been arranged for cadets in the Kahler School away from the home hospital are three months psychiatric nursing at one of the State Hospitals; two months tuberculosis nursing at Glen Lake Sanitarium in Oak Terrace; three months rural nursing at Bemidji, Crookston or Grand Rapids; six weeks communicable disease nursing at Ancker Hospital in St. Paul...A general medical or a neurological service may also be arranged at St. Mary's here in Rochester...Among the courses offered senior cadets in the Kahler School are: assistant to the Science Instructor, assistant to the Health Adviser, assistant head nurse in charge of a unit, assistant to the night supervisors and assistant in various operating room services...[15]

The senior cadets were invaluable, filling in for thousands of nurses who had volunteered to serve in the military. "The senior cadet nurses accepted the responsibilities of some of those nurses and proved they were qualified to fill the vacated positions."[16] "Of the 436 students enrolled in 1943 in the Kahler School of Nursing, 349 participated in the Cadet Nurse Corps program."[17] The cadets were professional in appearance as well as in performance. For example, the cadet's summer uniform was gray seersucker with a white purse, and lightweight felt hats were to be worn as well as white or black shoes. There was a high demand for white gloves, in the Rochester stores the first few days of the program.[18]

The U.S. Cadet Nurse Corps provided an intensive educational program that brought thousands of nurses into wartime service.

The Bolton Act stipulated that there "shall be no discrimination...on account of race, creed or color."[19] As a result, nursing schools across the United States soon began to open their doors to diverse applicants. Saint Marys School of Nursing and the Kahler School of Nursing were leaders in this regard; when the program began in July 1943, both admitted numerous Japanese-Americans who had been forced into internment camps by the United States Goverment because of the war. Fumiye Yoshida Lee, R.N., came to Saint Marys School of Nursing from the Minidoka Relocation Center in Idaho. "...It was a fantastic opportunity to be accepted at one of the best hospitals in the United States to work

Cadets displayed their flag at Saint Marys Hospital. They wore standard-issue wool coats in the Minnesota winter.

with the Mayo Clinic doctors...[The program] opened doors to us when we were facing discrimination."[20] Teruko Yamashita Okimoto, R.N., recalled her cadet experience that provided her with an opportunity to escape the interment camp and become a nurse:

For three years I had lived with my family of seven members in one little room in a city of barracks. Leaving for the outside world, alone, was a little frightening. Arriving in Rochester, I was overwhelmed... The standard of education [there] was the highest, the instructors were excellent, and the medical care, the finest!

Japanese Americans were not the only ones to take advantage of the cadet program. During the war, the training programs in Rochester prepared more than 2,000 cadet nurses for service to their country—951 at Saint Marys Hospital School of Nursing and 1,052 at the Kahler School of Nursing.[21] Afterward, each faculty member received a certificate recognizing their important contribution:

As an instructor, your influence will be reflected in each of the young women to whom you have imparted your skill, knowledge and wisdom. Through them you have cared for hundreds of patients. You have produced the graduate nurses of tomorrow who will be a vital factor in the public health of the country and the world.[22]

Saint Marys Hospital was a leader in admitting Japanese-American women into the cadet nursing program. Teruko Yamashita Okimoto, R.N., had been interned with her family at a civilian relocation camp before coming to Rochester.

The *Alumnae Quarterly* and *The Link*

As graduate nurses left Rochester for military service in other parts of the country or overseas, alumnae publications *Alumnae Quarterly*, from Saint Marys school and *The Link* from the Kahler school, kept them connected to their roots. The connection was important. They could not only keep up with news in Rochester but could also share their own experiences with friends and former colleagues. Alumnae correspondents often commented on their time in Rochester and the influence it had on their lives. La Vern Hollister, R.N., and Myrtle Hanna, R.N., both of the Kahler Class of 1940, wrote from Hawaii immediately after the attack on Pearl Harbor, describing their work in a busy obstetrical department:

The first days following Pearl Harbor it was difficult to carry on our work due to the blackout regulations, especially in the delivery rooms and nursery. We often recalled our History of Nursing as we carried our little lanterns through the dark corridors. We actually felt like little Florence Nightingales.[23]

As in previous eras, the nurses brought Mayo methods and Mayo values wherever they went. Mabel Jensen, R.N., with the 36th General Hospital in France, described how she changed nursing practice:

In Dijon we set up another hospital where, at times, I was responsible for up to 200 patients...All of our patients were right from the battlefront... I initiated the use of a dressing cart with two corpsmen. The idea came with me from Colonial and Kahler Hospitals.[24]

Flexibility was an important Mayo value. From 2nd Lt. Jeanette Long, R.N., 26th General Hospital somewhere in North Africa, came one example of the nurses' adaptability to wartime realities:

...You should see us. We wore coveralls all the way out here, GI men's shoes and fatigue hats just like the soldiers wear. Nothing glamorous about us. Have pitched our tents on the side of another hill, a muddy one at that and call it home...The mud is pretty bad, thick clay that clings to your feet and makes you look like a small tractor. Our hospital is going up. It is going to be in tents, with a few Nisei huts for surgery, critically ill patients, etc...[25]

Alumnae relied on their training for the skills to care for patients, no matter what the circumstances. Among these were two "Kahler Girls" who became flight nurses. Lt. Rose Morrow, R.N., wrote of their experience, noting that she had traveled many miles since being in Rochester the previous August:

Miss Littleton [R.N.] and I are still together...and relieve the nurses bringing the patients from North Africa and India. We have been so busy we each make most of our

Margaret Hedges Schroeder, R.N., Kahler Class of 1934, served in this field hospital in Northern Africa.

trips alone. We fly to [America], which is 2,300 miles from here or an 18-hour trip. We are allowed 24 hours and then we dead head back and get ready for our next trip. It keeps us pretty tired but we do enjoy it so very much. The number of our patients varies. I have had as many as 27...Some of the boys have been waiting seven months in a hospital to go home and are they thankful! [26]

From 2nd Lt. Irene Doty, R.N., came another report:

...Our team has been with a British Hospital for several weeks [in North Africa] and that is an experience in itself...My training out at St. Mary's is very beneficial here and I'm so glad I have a specialty. Can give an IV anesthetic with ease now. [27]

The "Mayo Units" in the Pacific
While many Mayo physicians and Rochester nurses worked in France, Italy, and North Africa with various British and American hospital units, those with the 71st General Hospital remained at home or in training camps in the United States, waiting for orders. Finally the orders came, and in August 1943, 71st General Hospital was divided into two equal-sized station

hospitals: the 233rd under the direction of Dr. Chuck Mayo and the 237th under the leadership of his Mayo Clinic colleague, James Priestley, M.D. [28] Members of both hospital units would soon travel by rail to Camp Stoneman in California, to await further directions.

Soon after New Year's Day of 1944, orders arrived and the two Mayo units boarded the S.S. *Nieuw Amsterdam*, a luxury liner converted into a troop ship, destined for New Guinea. After fourteen days at sea, zigzagging across the Pacific Ocean behind blackout curtains, they arrived in Sydney, Australia. [29] A month later, minus the nurses, whom Dr. Chuck ordered to remain in Australia until the 233rd and 237th hospitals could be built in the jungles of New Guinea, the physicians, officers, and enlisted men set sail for their final destination.

Nurses arrived in New Guinea in mid 1944. All the facilities of the 71st General Hospital, where they worked, had to be built from scratch.

Courtesy History Center of Olmsted County

The Mayo units served "at the foot of cloud-topped jungle mountains," recalled one nurse.

In New Guinea, each hospital had to be built from scratch, the doctors pitching in to help.[30] With seventy-nine American military nurses already Japanese prisoners of war at the Santo Tomas and Los Banos internment camps in the Philippines, Dr. Chuck and Dr. Priestley took no chances with their nurses' safety.[31] Only when the hospital buildings and nurses' barracks were ready in mid May were the nurses of the 233rd and 237th station hospitals allowed to set sail.[32]

Once in New Guinea, the nurses joined the two Mayo units "at the foot of cloud-topped jungle mountains and provided the first treatment for casualties evacuated by air from the campaign against Japan.[33] By this time, the hospitals had wooden buildings with separate quarters for officers and nurses. According to Lt. Phyllis Bohleen, R.N., who worked with the Minnesota team, surgery at the hospital in New Guinea was "almost like in an operating room at home, [with both] plumbing and electricity [although both would] get a bit temperamental" at times.[34]

One physician described the units' work saying, "The patients would come in waves. When there was action going on up north, there would be a lot of casualties...the nurses, like everyone else on the medical teams, would be busy around the clock.[35] When they weren't caring for the wounded, the teams turned their attention to patients with infectious diseases. In the rain forest, "dysentery...malaria and scrub typhus were common."[36] Mosquito-borne malaria was a particularly vexing problem and the staff members themselves were not immune. One of the nurses working with the 233rd hospital developed cerebral malaria. According to Delmar Gillespie, M.D., "Everyone knew her and we were all concerned...We gave her massive doses of intravenous Atabrine...and, by gad, she survived! And she wouldn't go home; she stayed there with us!"[37] A reunion publication in 1962 offered this recollection:

In New Guinea: Will you ever forget?
- Our first glimpse of the jungle?
- The mud, malaria and mosquitoes, the endless variety of bugs, bugs, bugs?...

- The mold of the jungle, scavenging for boxes, paint and air mattresses for our unyielding army cots?...
- The eternal shroud of the mosquito nets at night? The heat?
- Washing clothes in rain water trapped in helmets?"...[38]

Living in open barracks that were divided into individual cubicles, with latrines, showers, and laundry facilities all within their stockade, the nurses considered themselves pretty lucky. Nonetheless, they were still at war and far from home. To cope with their homesickness and the boredom that set in during slow days, the nurses turned to gardening, movies, dances, and music. As Beatrice DeLue, R.N., who served in Nadzab and later in the Philippines, recalled:

We had a little phonograph, and most of us brought a record from home... There were movies quite often. We'd sit on the bomb crates to watch them...We had a building for dances...and you could play cards in there... Some of the nurses had their parents send seeds for flowers, so we had a pathway of flowers going around the place.[39]

The social activities were important, both for the nurses and for other hospital staff. Between periods of intense activity when new patients came in, nurses, physicians, and other members of the unit found themselves with many hours to fill.[40]

On October 15, 1944, the 233rd Station Hospital was designated the 247th General Hospital.[41] In 1945, after the Pacific campaign moved northward, the hospitals were reassigned to the Philippines to treat casualties from the Okinawa campaign. There, after a miserable, rainy and muddy week, the 247th set up near Clarke Field (about eighty miles north of Manila) and the 237th Station Hospital relocated to Batangas.[42] At Clarke Field, in addition to treating trauma cases, physicians and nurses treated hundreds of soldiers for syphilis and gonorrhea brought on by their farewell flings in Marseilles. Penicillin was the drug of choice.[43]

Penicillin, discovered by Sir Alexander Fleming in 1929, was widely produced by American pharmaceutical companies during World War II. Mayo Clinic had early access to the drug for investigational purposes, and in 1942, Wallace Herrell, M.D., and his Mayo Clinic colleagues reported on the drug's clinical use for "inhibiting the growth of streptococci and staphylococci, as well as anaerobic organisms."[44] By the 1940s, penicillin was now considered a wonder drug. On July 16, 1945, Sir Alexander Fleming was honored at Mayo Clinic Foundation House for his far-reaching discovery.[45] Penicillin would revolutionize medical care in the decades that followed.

Duty in the South Pacific alternated between intense activity when wounded and ill patients arrived at the Mayo-sponsored hospitals and long periods of waiting. Socializing, movies, dances, and gardening helped fill the quiet times.

Helen Keller Lauds Nurses Enrolled in State Corps

Members of Company D, nurse corps of the Minnesota State Guard, at their regular meeting at the armory last night had as their honor guest and speaker, Miss Helen Keller, accompanied by her companion, Miss Polly Thomson.

"This is a sweet moment for me," Miss Keller began, "surrounded by brave young women full of a purpose that gives meaning and dignity to life. In you I sense the ideals which have made and will keep America a mighty power for good.

"What a splendid opportunity you have to embody one of those ideals—the highest creative service!

"Yesterday I realized this as never before while witnessing two brain operations. Full of admiration, I learned with what courage, poise, speed and fortitude the nurses executed countless orders upon which the patients' lives literally hung from minute to minute. In a glorious sense nurses are soldiers ever on the alert.

"As members of Company D you will participate in an unparalleled effort to vindicate the liberties and blessings of democracy. As daughters of America I know you will incarnate in yourselves the principles and practices that alone can bring about the triumph of light and civilization over barbarism and darkness. Go forward to the new womanhood that shall rise with healing in its hands for all the nations."

Internationally renowned author and humanitarian, Helen Keller, was a loyal patient of Mayo Clinic. While in Rochester, she addressed the Company D Nurse Corps of the Minnesota State Guard, "In you I sense the ideals which have made and will keep America a mighty power for good."

On the Home Front

During the war years, the need for nurses in civilian hospitals was as real as that in the military. With the boom in industrial and public health nursing, as well as the employment of women in manufacturing plants and other war-related jobs, fewer nurses chose hospital nursing as a career path.[46] Meanwhile, advances in anesthesia administration and a revolution in thoracic and cardiovascular surgery only increased the demand for skilled nurses who could provide specialty care for patients before, during, and after an operation.[47]

In Rochester, Mayo Clinic and its affiliated hospitals, already desperately short of nurses, now needed even more as "one of the nation's preeminent thoracic surgeons," O. Theron Clagett, M.D., operated on hundreds of adults and children in life-saving chest surgeries.[48] Nurses were essential members of Dr. Clagett's team—some preparing patients for surgery, others circulating and scrubbing during the complicated thoracic cases, and still others observing and caring for patients after the procedure. In this era before intensive care, when the recovery room was just being introduced in many hospitals, it soon became evident that these critically ill patients needed special care by nurses who were adept at using such equipment as oxygen tents, suction catheters, and chest tubes.

As patient admission rates continued to rise in other areas besides surgery, there was a persistent need for additional hospital beds. In 1941, the Medical Building (later named the Francis Building) opened at Saint Marys, increasing the total capacity of the hospital to 868 beds and providing new facilities for the departments of medicine, pediatrics, dietetics, pharmacy, and obstetrics.[49]

In addition to hospital nurses, Saint Marys needed nurses for the new Home Nursing Service, developed in 1943 by Sister Eymard Tracy, R.N. Based on her educational and practical experience in public health nursing at Henry Street Settlement in New York City, she was convinced that Rochester's citizens would benefit from home visits. The service, operating in cooperation with the Rochester public health agencies, provided free home care to patients after discharge from Saint Marys.[50]

Caring Healers in Pediatrics

With the opening of the Francis Building, the growing specialty of pediatrics, assigned to the sixth floor, finally had the square footage it needed, including "space for both small and older children, a real nursery—for those less than one year of age—a formula room, a playroom and a sun-porch for visitors..."[51]

In this area, nurses learned and practiced the new specialty, paying specific attention to the psychological and developmental needs of infants, toddlers, and young children, as well as to their physical needs. Members of an interdisciplinary team participated in the care, with staff members using their imagination to relate to the children. "Orderlies convinced children that the wheelchairs were horses," and

by the 1950s, when the emphasis on space age technology was sweeping the world, anesthesiologists and nurse anesthetists "applied imaginary space masks over their small patients' faces for the initial inductions."[52] In 1960, the employee publication described the admission protocol for the unit, noting that, "...the children are usually taken to the playroom to help them adjust more easily."[53]

Holistic care was the norm in pediatrics. Christmas was especially exciting as pediatric patients were encouraged to put their shoes out for Saint Nicholas.[54] For years, the Franciscan Sisters ensured that Santa arrived on the wards with Sister Columba Michalec, a chubby and jolly sister, the first person to play the role. Sister Antoine Murphy, R.N., recalled how the tradition evolved:

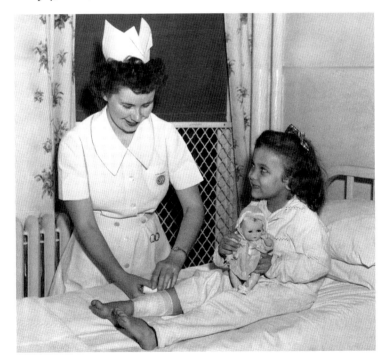

The post-war "Baby Boom" accelerated the development of pediatrics as a medical specialty. Nurses at Saint Marys Hospital (left), and the Kahler Hospitals (right), made caring for children a priority.

The children had their Christmas party in that playroom and Santa would come skiing down the hill! And, of course, he'd go through quite a few antics and he'd spill his toys and fall! Then he'd finally get to the door, and there would be a long pause, and then Dr. Roger Kennedy, in a Santa Claus suit, would play the 'inside' Santa [as] he knew the children by name.[55]

Solutions for the Nursing Shortage

As early as 1941, the Office of Civilian Defense and the American Red Cross urged hospitals and nursing schools to cooperate in the training of volunteer nurses' aides.[56] Early in 1942, Saint Marys opened its doors to American Red Cross volunteers and "Grey Ladies"—both of whom could help nurses keep the hospital running efficiently.[57] In pediatrics, Girl Scout volunteers, called "Pinafore Girls" because of their aprons, gave their time and effort.[58] Working five hours a week, on weekends or after school, the young volunteers helped the nurses by rocking, feeding, and playing with the small patients.

During the summers of 1944-1947, the teaching Sisters of Saint Francis assisted the hospital staff.[59] Sister Amadeus Klein recalled those days, noting, "There was no escort service, no lab collection for specimens, no pharmacy and no central service until the late 1950s, so these duties were assigned to nurses' aides."[60] The practice was typical of that in hospitals throughout the nation.

Left: This recruitment brochure emphasized the scientific as well as the caregiving dimensions of nursing. Right: Teenage volunteers, nicknamed "Pinafore Girls" for the apron they wore, helped alleviate he shortage of nurses.

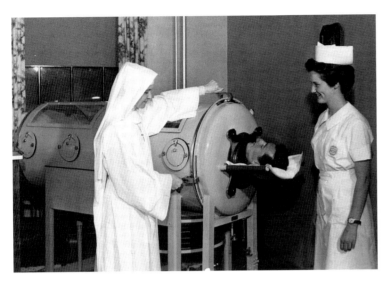

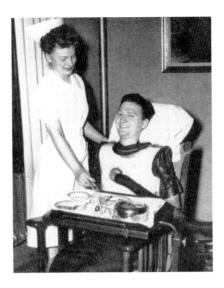

Left: Before the Salk vaccine, polio was a major health threat. Dave Madden contracted polio in 1948 and lived for 16 years in an iron lung at Saint Marys Hospital. **Right:** *A portable respirator provided him with limited mobility. Sister Regina Buskowiak, R.N., far left, oversaw his care and that of many other polio patients.*

The Polio Epidemics

In the 1940s, epidemics of poliomyelitis (first called infantile paralysis because of its tendency to attack small children) added to the demand for nurses, further complicating the nursing shortage.[61] Since 1916, when there was a large outbreak of the infection in the United States, seasonal polio epidemics had recurred throughout the country—mostly in the summer months. The horrific virus, attacking nerves of the spinal cord, left thousands of children and adults crippled; many others died.

The polio outbreaks of the 1940s were particularly serious. In 1943, Ethel Nash, R.N., wrote to her Rochester nurse colleagues, asking for information on any research being done at the Clinic on poliomyelitis.[62] She was working in Morenci, Arizona, where she feared an epidemic, and wrote, "I find I am completely out of date in my knowledge of it. My only source of information is a manila folder Miss Durland had us prepare as students of communicable diseases..."[63]

TEAMWORK

"Between July 5 and October 11, 1946, St. Mary's Hospital admitted '110 patients for the treatment of polio'...Frequently there were three patients in respirators, requiring the services of nine nurses in a 24-hour period...One or two Kahler Senior Cadets came at a time for a two-week service over a period of several months. We were particularly pleased when two of these students returned on their day off to give volunteer services..."

Ethel Nash was sure that her colleagues in Rochester would know the latest science related to polio, and she was correct. Only a year earlier, Sister Elizabeth Kenny, R.N., the famous "polio nurse" from Australia who treated patients by using hot packs and stretching affected limbs rather than splinting them, had traveled to Minnesota and lectured to the Mayo Clinic staff on her revolutionary procedures.[64] By 1943, the "Kenny Method" had become standard treatment for polio at Mayo-affiliated hospitals. At Saint Marys in the 1940s, "every available wool and cotton blanket" was run under hot water and wrung out, then wrapped around the legs of the patients with polio.[65]

From 1945 to 1949, large epidemics of polio occurred in the United States with an average of more than 20,000 cases a year. When the epidemics raged, Saint Marys had many polio patients as it was the only hospital in the region with facilities capable of dealing with major outbreaks of contagious diseases.[66] The summer of 1946

71

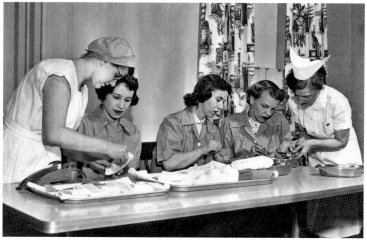

When the polio vaccine became available, mass dispensations ensured that people received the protective drug as soon as possible. Nurses at Rochester Methodist Hospital taught members of the hospital auxiliary the proper techniques of filling vaccination syringes.

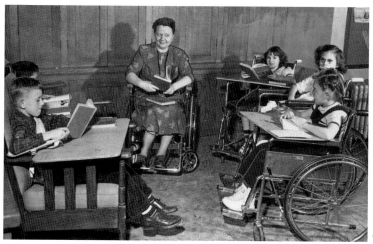

Courtesy Minnesota Historical Society

Rochester Public Schools teacher Ida Staehling, herself a polio survivor, taught children in the polio ward of Saint Marys Hospital.

was especially difficult as the epidemic leapfrogged unpredictably across the country, and patients came to Mayo Clinic from nearby states and Canada in addition to local and regional communities.[67]

Constant vigilance, teamwork, and technical proficiency in managing the iron lungs, became hallmarks of the nurses' work. As polio paralyzed the respiratory system, these iron lung were negative pressure respirators that allowed patients to breathe. Between July 5 and October 11, 1946, Saint Marys Hospital admitted 110 patients for the treatment of polio. Frequently there were three patients in iron lungs, requiring the services of nine nurses in a 24-hour period. One or two Kahler Senior Cadets came at a time for a two-week service over a period of several months and sometimes these students returned on their day off to volunteer services."[68]

In 1949, the epidemic was still present. Since the first of June, 108 patients had been admitted to the hospital for poliomyelitis. The most seriously ill patients were placed in iron lungs and other patients whom could not move their arms or legs, went to the Isolation Ward.[69] In the August 9 Minutes of the Coordinating

Committee, Sister Domitilla reported on the polio situation stating, "[There were] 21 patients in isolation—18 of them with polio. To date, dismissals have been frequent enough that new admissions have been possible."[70] By September 5, the polio situation had become the polio problem at Saint Marys. There were thirteen patients in the Isolation Department and 35 post-polios admitted to the first floor.[71]

The nurses needed help. Providing care for polio patients was both physically and emotionally exhausting. The hospital was already short of nurses, and public health officials were predicting that the high incidence of polio would not subside until late October. According to the newspapers, hospital authorities sent out an urgent appeal for graduate nurses, stating, "Any graduate nurse who can give a few hours a day for a period of a week to two months is urged to contact the nursing department or the personnel department...immediately."[72]

By October 31, 1949, the epidemic was subsiding and the Coordinating Committee was exploring the possibility of transferring some of the post-polio children to pediatrics where classes would be conducted by a teacher from the Rochester Public School system.[73]

As had been true in past epidemics, the Mayo response to this crisis was a team effort. Six years later, when Jonas Salk's polio vaccine became available to the public, the polio epidemics ended. As a result, when the new Domitilla Building opened the next year, the rehabilitation space planned for polio patients would be used to house patients recovering from strokes and other injuries.[74]

Rochester School of Practical Nurses and Homemakers
The post-World War II era brought new challenges to the nursing profession and to nursing in Rochester. Several factors contributed to these challenges: the availability of Hill Burton and private funding spurred the growth of hospitals across the nation; the demand for hospital care was at an all-time high; and thousands of nurses returned

Margaret Raymond (left) and Michon Laganiere, L.P.N., discussed patient care at the Renal Clinic in the Mayo Building.

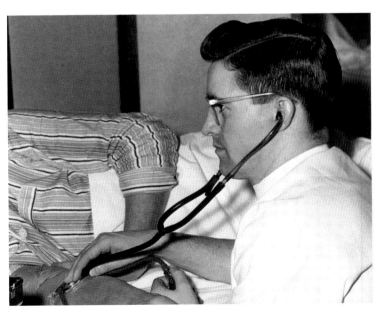

Charles Henry, L.P.N., Class of 1952, was the first male student in the Rochester School of Practical Nursing and Homemaking at Saint Marys Hospital.

to their homes to raise families, trying to put the war behind them. It was also the period of the "Baby Boom," and in the late 1940s and 1950s most women chose to deliver their babies in hospitals. That fact, in concert with a rise in heart disease, cancer, and stroke, meant that more patients were being hospitalized.

In the late 1940s and early '50s, addressing the nursing shortage was an ongoing challenge. Restructuring the professional nurses' role offered a feasible option, and team nursing, with professional nurses gradually shifting from direct care to managing licensed practical nurses and auxiliary personnel became the norm.[75] At Saint Marys, in an attempt to allow the R.N. more specific responsibilities, Sister Domitilla founded the Rochester School of Practical Nursing and Homemakers, appointing Rose Peterka, R.N., director, and Sister Generose Gervais as co-director and instructor. The school

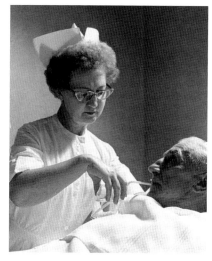  

From left: Melba Zerck, R.N., Rochester Methodist Hospital; Mary Bauer, R.N.; Patricia Soukup, R.N., with student Gloria Joynt, R.N., Saint Marys Hospital.

admitted the first class of students in January 1948.[76] Following an orientation period, a series of lectures on nursing principles and procedures, nutrition in health and illness, and applied science, as well as supervised practice of the care in medical and surgical patients, children, mothers, newborn infants, and the older adult completed the one-year course of study.[77]

Upon graduation, practical nurses were eligible to write the state board examination for practical licensure and upon successful completion, qualified to care for subacute, convalescent, and chronic patients of all age groups, under the supervision of a registered nurse or a licensed physician.[78] In Rochester, licensed practical nurses would soon become essential members of the nursing team—a team devoted to the patient as the priority of care. Practical nurses developed their own traditions within the overall culture of Mayo Clinic and Saint Marys Hospital. This pride was reflected in the school's emblem that contained a cross surmounted by the school's motto, *"Serviam"* which means, "I will serve."[79]

Key Collaborations

From the earliest days of the Mayo brothers' practice in Rochester, physicians and nurses had collaborated in scientific discovery and the application of research to patient care. With an increasing emphasis on medical research as the twentieth century progressed, Rochester nurses became more involved in clinical trials.

In the late 1940s, for example, Sister Pantaleon Navratil, R.N., provided nursing supervision for a clinical trial that led to the discovery of cortisone. In September 1948, Philip Hench, M.D., and Edward Kendall, Ph.D., who had been conducting research on adrenal hormones for several years, used "Compound E" (cortisone) on a rheumatoid arthritis patient with astonishing results, less muscle stiffness and soreness. In April 1949, they released the results to their Mayo colleagues and in the following year, Drs. Kendall and Hench received the Nobel Prize for this work. Well versed in the Mayo precepts of collaboration and cooperation, Dr. Hench shared some of the prize money with his valuable colleague in recognition of

Sister Pantaleon's contributions to the project. Because Sister Pantaleon could not accept money directly, Dr. Hench set up a travel fund for her to tour Europe for both professional and personal development.[80] John Mayne, M.D., a specialist in rheumatology and colleague of Dr. Hench, recalled that Sister Pantaleon "was absolutely wonderful, ran the clinical areas superbly and very ably assisted with clinical trials."[81]

Other nurses' roles in research were less visible but no less important. For example, Sister Antoine Murphy recalled setting up elaborate tubing for a renal patient when dialysis was introduced in an experimental attempt to save the life of a patient in the end stages

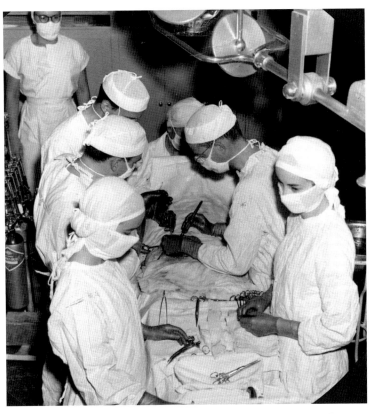

At Rochester Methodist Hospital, John Kirklin, M.D., and surgical colleagues performed the nation's first successful series of open-heart procedures, beginning with a five-year-old patient in 1955.

Mayo Clinic staff consultants Edward Kendall, Ph.D., (left) and Philip Hench, M.D., shared the 1950 Nobel Prize for the development of cortisone.

of kidney failure.[82] Others assisted in caring for patients who enrolled in various clinical trials.

Participation in state-of-the-art medical care was not new to nurses affiliated with Mayo Clinic. By 1950, when John Kirklin, M.D., joined Mayo's staff, innovations in cardiothoracic surgery were the norm, leading to the world's first series of open-heart surgeries using the Mayo-Gibbon heart-lung bypass machine.[83] All of these surgeries required interdisciplinary collaboration; a typical cardiothoracic surgical team included surgeons, nurses, cardiopulmonary bypass and laboratory technicians, pharmacists, anesthesiologists, and respiratory therapists.[84] On March 22, 1955, the first patient to benefit from the new machine occurred when Dr. Kirklin's team operated on a five-year-old girl at Rochester Methodist Hospital. Three members of the surgical team were nurses: Delores Miller, R.N., Shirley Reusser, R.N., and Elizabeth Goodwyne, R.N.[85]

Incorporation as Rochester Methodist Hospital
The innovative teamwork taking place on Dr. Kirklin's team in 1955 was typical of that occurring throughout Mayo hospitals and was part of a new administrative structure initiated only a year earlier. In 1954, the Kahler Hospitals and the Kahler School of Nursing were sold and incorporated as Rochester Methodist Hospital.[86]

Now, in addition to the underlying principles of the Franciscan Sisterhood and those specific to the Mayos themselves, Methodist values would provide a foundation for patient care. Chief among these were a growing emphasis on strong community engagement and the transition to a not-for-profit philosophy.

To reinforce the new identity while respecting the heritage of nursing education, the Kahler Hospital School of Nursing was renamed the Methodist-Kahler School of Nursing. Harold Mickey, administrator of Rochester Methodist Hospital, and Esther Roesti, R.N., Director of Nursing, shared adaptability to new ideas, which made possible many improvements at Methodist-Kahler School of Nursing within a short period of time. The number of faculty increased and the school began to focus on student learning rather

As more men entered nursing, the Methodist-Kahler School of Nursing opened a dormitory for male students. It was named Christopher Graham Hall in honor of Christopher Graham, M.D., an early partner of the Doctors Mayo and brother of Edith Graham, R.N. Dr. Graham (second from left) attended the dedication ceremony in 1950.

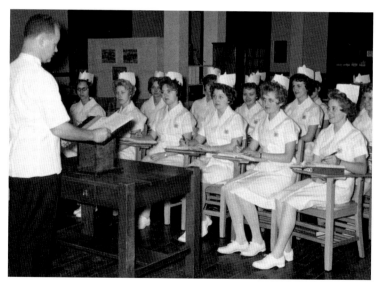

Methodist-Kahler students listened to a lecture about pharmacology from a pharmacist.

than on apprenticeship for service to the hospital.[87] For the students at Methodist-Kahler School of Nursing, the most visible indication of change would be the new initials embroidered on their winter capes, while the focus of their education remained steadfast. The patient's needs would always come first.[88]

Innovations in Care

Throughout the United States, the growth of hospitals and dramatic changes in technology and science, combined with an emphasis on the new concept of progressive patient care proposed in the nursing literature, led to innovations in the design of facilities and the delivery of nursing care[89] Progressive patient care involved the "organization of facilities, services and staff around the medical and nursing needs of the patient."[90] In Rochester, Minnesota, where building renovation and construction were constant, progressive patient care resonated with the time-honored philosophy that the patient was the center of care.

From special care units for the critically ill, patients would move to step-down units and on to home care.[91] Of these three aspects, the most exciting for doctors and nurses dealing with increasingly complex and critically ill hospitalized patients was the idea of the intensive care unit.[92] Development of the intensive care unit addressed multiple issues in the 1950s: the persistent shortage of nurses in hospitals throughout the country; the need for round-the-clock observation of postoperative neurosurgery, cardiac surgical, and trauma patients; the introduction of new machines and monitors; and the doubling in size and change of configuration of hospitals (wards closed and semiprivate rooms became the norm). To group the most critically ill patients in one place under the care of nurses trained specifically to care for them simply made sense.[93]

Rochester nurses supported this idea from the start; under the leadership of Sister Amadeus Klein and Sister Mary Brigh Cassidy, began plans for a neurosciences intensive care unit as early as 1955. However, because Dr. Kirklin and the team had moved their heart

Saint Marys Hospital was a national leader in the development of intensive care units.

surgery program to Saint Marys Hospital, the need for a cardiac nursing intensive care unit became acute.[94] Indeed, Dr. Kirklin and his colleagues needed nurses trained in the care of the critically ill to provide a high degree of nursing skill and constant attention to patients in the first postoperative days.[95] Thus, while plans for both units proceeded, a cardiac surgical intensive care unit was the priority. It opened in the spring of 1958.[96]

The second intensive care unit—for neurological and neurosurgical patients—opened a few months later located just off the main neurology and neurosurgery ward.[97] There, nurses who specialized in neuro-anatomy, oxygen therapy, respirators, and the use of hypothermia blankets provided round-the-clock observation and care for critically ill postoperative neurosurgical patients and those suffering from serious neurological conditions, including Guillain-Barre syndrome and subarachnoid hemorrhage.[98] Using their advanced training in clinical assessment, nurses served as vigilant guardians for their

In 1966, Rochester Methodist Hospital opened a new, state-of-the-art building. Esther Roesti, R.N., Director of Nursing (center) helped lead the project, along with Executive Director Harold Mickey (left) and David Trites, M.D., Director of Research (right).

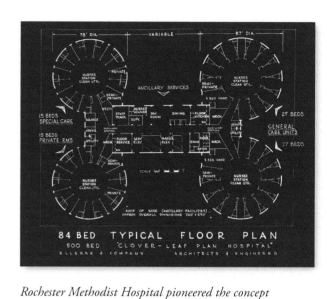

Rochester Methodist Hospital pioneered the concept of the radial nursing unit, an innovative floor plan later adopted by many hospitals and used in the new Rochester Methodist Hospital.

patients, recognizing early signs of patient deterioration and providing skilled intervention in the new high-tech environment.

At the same time, nurses at Rochester Methodist Hospital were also participating in designing and implementing an intensive care unit for postoperative cardiac patients.[99] The unit was designed in the round and was known as the "circular unit" when it opened in December 1957.[100] The nurses' station was at the center of twelve patient rooms with all rooms visible to the nurses. Under the leadership of Nurse Coordinator Jeannette Vidic, R.N., and Head Nurse Joanne Skinner, R.N., the circular unit proved successful, providing for continuous patient observation from the nurses' desk and eliminating the amount of walking a nurse had to do to check on patients.[101]

By 1960, Rochester Methodist Hospital was planning for six floors of four circular units each built on top of a rectangular base in which administrative offices, operating rooms, laboratories, and ancillary

services would be located. According to one report, "The circular unit, under study during the past three years at Methodist Hospital, has been found to offer such advantages in patient care that this concept of building form has been made the basis of preliminary architectural planning for a new Methodist Hospital to be built at a future date."[102]

By 1964, Saint Marys also had established a general medical intensive care unit, planned in part by Sister Mary Brigh. The six two-bed rooms with a central nursing station were equipped with new heart monitoring devices as well as oxygen and suction equipment. In 1974, Saint Marys opened a cardiac intensive care unit supervised by Sister Henry (Charlotte) Dusbabek, R.N.[103] Both the intensive care unit and cardiac care unit would foster dramatic changes in the delivery of patient care.

These changes in hospital design were more than architectural. In the intensive and coronary care units, nurses assumed new and advanced responsibilities. For example, nurses became adept at reading electrocardiograms and interpreting cardiac arrhythmias, defibrillating patients when necessary, and performing cardiopulmonary resuscitation.

The expanding role of the nurse was happening across the nation. As Lawrence Meltzer, M.D., a cardiologist at Presbyterian Hospital in Philadelphia, predicted in 1962 when he opened one of the first cardiac care units there, the role of the nurse in these units would be different.[104] In Rochester and throughout the nation, a scientific team approach was being advocated. As Dr. Meltzer described it, "the nurse, by definition of her responsibilities [would be a] vital member" of that scientific team.[105] One example of this teamwork occurred at Rochester Methodist Hospital on March 10, 1969, when orthopedic surgeon Mark Conventry, M.D., and colleagues performed the first total hip replacement surgery authorized by the Food and Drug Administration.[106]

Teamwork and Problem Solving in Vietnam

A world away from Minnesota in Vietnam, teamwork was essential to the provision of care for injured soldiers. Elwood Wilkins, R.N., a graduate of the Nurse Anesthesia Program in the Mayo School of Health Sciences, was a vital member of a military surgical team whose mission it was to treat U.S. troops wounded in the fight against the Viet Cong. Aware that nurse anesthetists were desperately needed there, Wilkins enlisted in the U.S. Army on June 2, 1966—the day he graduated as a nurse anesthetist.[107] U.S. troops had been sent to Vietnam only a year earlier, after a sustained U.S. aerial bombing campaign on North Vietnam in March 1965—the United States' response to the attack on two of its destroyers in what would be known as the Gulf of Tonkin incident.[108]

Elwood Wilkins, R.N., far right, enlisted in the Army the day he graduated from the Nurse Anesthesia Program in 1966. This photo shows him on active duty with surgical colleagues in Vietnam.

On the ground, jungle warfare was the norm, and Elwood Wilkins spent a year in one of the busiest evacuation hospitals in Vietnam. Reflecting upon his experiences:

[It was] not uncommon to have 100 casualties at a time...and surgeons wore flak jackets under their gowns...[working with] no running water, no ventilators and limited supplies...Mayo taught me to do things the right way...In Vietnam, we practiced jungle anesthesia, you make do with what you've got...Mayo made me confident...the Army made me ultra-confident.[109]

Elwood Wilkins had to rely on what he had learned in Rochester. Teamwork and problem solving were just part of the job. His experience was reminiscent of Mayo nurses in earlier wars who relied on Mayo Clinic values and methods to get them through. There were many other Mayo-trained nurses that served in the dense brush of jungle war and stateside. As caring healers for thousands of military recruits, they will not be forgotten.[110]

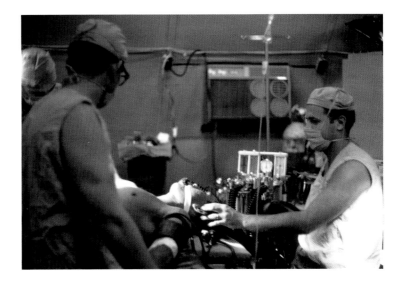

A New Era

By the late 1960s, transformative change was under way in nursing education throughout the United States. Several factors fueled the change: the dramatic growth of specialized nursing units, the evolution of new professional roles for nurses, and the growing emphasis on the B.S.N. (bachelor of science in nursing) degree as the entry level into the profession. In 1967, aware that national nursing organizations had endorsed the trend of moving general educational programs out of hospitals and into colleges, universities, and junior colleges, leaders of Saint Marys and Rochester Methodist announced that both hospitals would close their nursing schools in 1970; Rochester State Junior College would begin a two-year associate degree program in nursing. According to the announcement:

...As we viewed the future of our own school in relation to these trends, the presence of the Junior College in Rochester, combined with the outstanding clinical facilities in the city, seemed to offer the possibility of establishing an Associate Degree program in this city. A decision was made, therefore,

As part of a national trend, both Mayo-affiliated hospitals closed their nursing schools in 1970. The commitment to nursing education, however, continued in new and innovative ways.

The first nursing graduates from the new nursing program at Rochester State Junior College received their pins at commencement ceremonies in 1971.

to begin such a program in 1968 under the auspices of the Rochester State Junior College. Rochester Methodist Hospital, St. Mary's Hospital, and other health agencies in Rochester will be utilized for the students' clinical experience. This means that the two diploma schools in Rochester admitted their last freshman classes in the fall of 1967. These classes will be graduated in 1970.[111]

The Methodist-Kahler School issued its 3,827th diploma and the Saint Marys School of Nursing issued its 3,865th diploma before closing.[112]

In a letter written to the alumni, just prior to the closing of the Methodist-Kahler School of Nursing, Director Eleanor Smith, R.N., who had led the school since 1957, emphasized the school's impact, noting, "While the school itself is closing, we know that its influence will long continue. The ideals that it has stood for are perpetuated by those who attended here..."[113] Sister Mary Brigh of Saint Marys agreed, "In no way do we interpret the closing of the school as an end, but as a new direction that best meets the needs of a contemporary society... Certain values never change."[114] Both leaders were correct—Mayo ideals and values would endure, and nursing in Rochester would take new directions as it met the challenges of specialization and integration.

For much of the twentieth century, crisply starched caps were a distinctive part of a nurse's uniform. As with pins, nursing schools developed their own unique style of caps, a point of professional pride. Students received their caps after a probationary period, signifying acceptance by the school and readiness to begin hospital training. Starting in the 1960s and '70s, changing styles, concerns about sanitation, and the entrance of more men into nursing led to the formal uniform, including the cap, being replaced by scrubs.

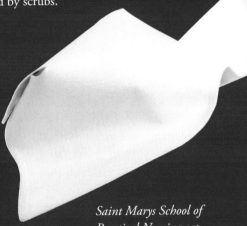

The pin of the Saint Marys School of Practical Nursing featured a cross, symbolizing trust in God and in one another, as well as the school motto, "Serviam," which means "To Serve." Gold rays, extending from the cross and motto, represented a life of service to people throughout the world.

The pin of the Kahler-Methodist School of Nursing featured the Staff of Aesculapius, symbol of medicine, a blend of Pattee and Maltese crosses, and the lamp associated with Florence Nightingale, which represented nursing.

The pin of the Saint Marys School of Nursing featured a shield, a symbol of protection for the patient in the hands of a nurse. The pin also included a blue cross, a symbol trust in God and each other, the letters N.T.S. for the school's original name, Nurses Training School, along with the school motto, "Sincere et Constanter," which means "Sincerity and Dependability."

Saint Marys School of Practical Nursing cap

Methodist-Kahler School of Nursing cap

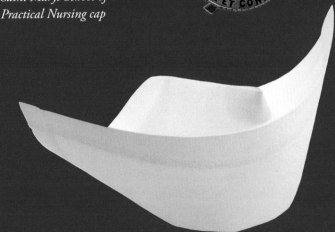

Saint Marys School of Nursing cap

Bike riding

Student choir at the dedication of Rochester Methodist Hospital

High Tea

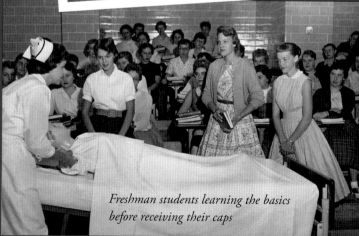

Freshman students learning the basics
before receiving their caps

Formal dances

Methodist-Kahler Students participate in the Capping and Candle Lighting Ceremony.

Students at Mass in the Saint Marys Hospital Chapel

Students at the May Crowning ceremony, an annual event where a crown of flowers was placed on a statue of the Virgin Mary.

Saint Marys School of Practical Nursing and Methodist-Kahler Graduation

ENDNOTES

1   Martha Thevoz, "The American Hospital of Paris," *The Link* (November, 1940): 14-15.

2   A review of letters in *The Link* documents details of the nurses' assignments. In these letters, they often refer to meeting another "Kahler Girl."

3   Naval History and Heritage Command, "Oral History of the Pearl Harbor Attack, 7 December 1941, Lieutenant Ruth Erickson, NC, USN," www.history.navy.mil/faqs/faq66-3b.htm (accessed June 6, 2012).

4   Ibid. See also "M-K Grad Heads Nurse Corps," *The Link* (1962): 21. Mayo Historical Unit.

5   Teresa Opheim, "Mayo in the Pacific," *Mayo Alumnus* (Spring, 1990): 3-14. Reprint: Rochester. Mayo Historical Unit.

6   "General Hospital, Officered Largely by Doctors Here, To Be Called Soon," *Rochester Post-Bulletin* (Wednesday, December 16, 1942): 1-2. Reprint: Rochester. Mayo Historical Unit.

7   Martha Kentta, "Kahler Alumnae Tea," *The Link* (November 1942): 13.

8   Charles S. Mudgett, "Headquarters 237th Station Hospital." Mayo Historical Unit, "Historical Data," Station Hospitals 233 and 237 File.

9   "We Fought a War Too," *A Reunion* (June 30, 1962). Mayo Historical Unit. WWII Pamphlet File.

10 Methodist-Kahler Alumni Association, "A Look Back at the Cadet Nurse Corps," *The Drawsheet,* 8, 3 (February 1988): 3.

11 Philip A. Kalisch and Beatrice J. Kalisch, *American Nursing: A History,* 4th ed (Philadelphia: Lippincott Williams and Wilkins, 2004): 314-317.

12 *Appendix B,* Pub. L. No. 74, 78th Cong., (February 20, 1948): 29-52. Reprint: Rochester. Mayo Historical Unit, Saint Marys School of Nursing archives.

13 Methodist-Kahler Alumni Association, "A Look Back," 3.

14 Kalisch and Kalisch, *American Nursing.*

15 Lulu Saunders, *The Link* (November 1944): 5.

16 Methodist-Kahler Alumni Association, "A Look Back," 3. See also "Over 77,000 U.S. Nurses Volunteered for Service in WWII. Two Hundred and Thirty Died in Service, 16 Were Killed as a Result of Enemy Action," www.americanmilitarynursesinwwii.com (accessed June 6, 2012; site now discontinued).

17 Methodist-Kahler Alumni Association, "A Look Back," 1-3.

18 Methodist-Kahler Alumni Association, "A Look Back." See also Fern Sheick, *The Link* (May 1944).

19 *Appendix B,* Pub. L. No. 74, 78th Cong., 29.

20 Fumiye Yoshida Lee, R.N., Virginia Wentzel papers.

21 "Instructors Honored," *Rochester Post-Bulletin* (February 5, 1946). Reprint: Rochester. Mayo Historical Unit.

22 Ibid.

23 La Vern Hollister and Myrtle H. Hanna, "Letters and Excerpts from Letters," *The Link* (November 1942): 13.

24 "We Fought a War Too," *A Reunion.*

25 Alumnae, *The Link* (June 1943): 11-12.

26 "The Kahler School of Nursing Alumnae," *The Link* (March 1944): 8.

27 Irene Doty, *The Link* (1943): 12. Mayo Historical Unit.

28 Mayo Vignette, "World War II: Mayo Goes to New Guinea," *Mayo Alumnus,* 23, 2 (Spring 1987).

29 "We Fought a War Too," *A Reunion.*

30 Opheim, "Mayo in the Pacific." See also "Historical Data" in Station Hospital 233 and 237 File, Mayo Historical Unit; and "We Fought a War Too," *A Reunion.*

31 Elizabeth Norma and Sharon Elfried, "How Did They All Survive?: An Analysis of American Nurses' Experience in Japanese Prisoner-of-War Camps," *Nursing History Review,* 3 (1995): 105-127. See also Elizabeth Norman, *We Band of Angels: The Untold Story of American Nurses Trapped on Bataan by the Japanese* (New York: Pocket Books, 1999).

32 Opheim, "Mayo in the Pacific"; see also "Historical Data," Station Hospital 233 and 237 File; and "We Fought a War Too," *A Reunion.*

33 John Henderson, "A Brief History of the Army of the United States 71st General Hospital (The Mayo Unit)," (September 1996): 1-3. Mayo Historical Unit. See also "Famous Mayo Clinic Men Run NG Jungle Hospital," newspaper clipping reprint (n.d., no identification) in Dr. Chuck Mayo Folder, Olmsted Historical Society. The 233rd Station Hospital was positioned a few miles inland at Nadzab, and the 237th was positioned near an airstrip on the coast at Finschafen.

34 Virginia Safford Letters, Staff Memories. Reprint: Rochester. Mayo Historical Unit, Folder: Brown, Philip with Mayo Clinic Army Hospitals, WWII, MHU-0670.

35 Teresa Opheim, "Mayo in the Pacific," *The Mayo Alumnus* (Spring 1990): 7. Mayo Historical Unit.

36 Opheim, "Mayo in the Pacific," 7. See also See also "Historical Data" in Mayo Historical Unit Station Hospital 233 and 237 File, and "We Fought a War Too," *A Reunion.*

37 Opheim, "Mayo in the Pacific," 8.

38 "We Fought a War Too," *A Reunion.*

39 Opheim, "Mayo in the Pacific," 9.

40 Ibid., 8.

41 Beck, Historical, 1190. See also John Henderson, "A Brief History" (September 1996): 1-3. Mayo Historical Unit.

42 Philip W. Brown, "Mayo Clinic Army Hospitals, WWII," 33. Mayo Historical Unit, Box 2, MHU-0670.

43 Ibid. See also Dr. Chuck Mayo, Letters, Olmsted Historical Society.

44 Wallace E. Herrell, Dorothy H. Heilman, and H.L. Williams, "The Clinical Use of Penicillin," *Proceedings of the Staff Meetings of the Mayo Clinic,* 17, 29 (December 30, 1942): 609- 616.

45 D.C. Balfour, N.M. Keith, John Cameron, and Sir Alexander Fleming, "Remarks Made at the Dinner for Sir Alexander Fleming," Mayo Foundation House (July 16, 1945). Mayo Historical Unit, Folder Penicillin, MHU-0676.

46 For more on this, see Kalisch and Kalisch, *American Nursing,* 318-319. See also "Letters From Kahler Alumnae," *The Link* (1941-1945), describing their nursing work in industrial plants.

47 A.P. Naef, "The Mid-Century Revolution in Thoracic and Cardiovascular Surgery: Part 2," *Interactive Cardiovascular and Thoracic Surgery,* 2 (2003): 431.

48 Ibid., 36.

49 Philip K. Strand, *A Century of Caring, 1889-1989* (Rochester: Saint Marys Hospital, 1989).

50 "A Home Nursing Service," *News Bulletin, St. Mary's Hospital,* II, 9 (October 1943):1-5.

51 Linda D. Sorenson, R.N., "Pediatrics and the History of Mayo Foundation" (2012): 3.

52 "In Pediatrics Expect the Unexpected," *Mayovox* (December 24, 1960).

53 Ibid.

54 Ibid. See also Sister Antoine Murphy, interview by Adam Holland and Arlene Keeling, March 30, 2012. Transcript.

55 Ibid.

56 Kalisch and Kalisch, *American Nursing,* 300. See also "Training Program Announced for 100,000 Nurses' Aides," *Hospital Management,* 52 (September 1941): 44-45.

57 Sister Ellen Whelan, *Sisters' Story Part 2, Saint Marys Hospital—Mayo Clinic, 1939 to 1980* (Rochester: Mayo Foundation for Medical Education and Research, 2007): 60-61.

58 Strand, *A Century of Caring,* 57. See also Whelan, *The Sisters' Story, Part 2,* 60-61.

59 Sister Amadeus Klein, "Neurological, Neurosurgical Nursing: St. Mary's Hospital, Rochester Minnesota, 1947-1960," 1. Mayo Historical Unit, Saint Marys School of Nursing archives. Sister Amadeus Klein was supervisor of Neurology and Neurosurgical Nursing, 1950-58.

60 Ibid., 4.

61 Whelan, *The Sisters' Story Part 2,* 137. See also Lynn Dunphy, "The Steel Cocoon: Tales of the Nurses and Patients of the Iron Lung, 1929-1955," *Nursing History Review,* 9 (2001):3-33.

62 Ethel K Nash, Class of 1933, *The Link* (1943): 13.

63 Ibid. Ms. Gilberta Durland, R.N., was Director of the School of Nursing from 1949-1957. She was on the faculty for 35 years and was "warmly remembered in her various roles as instructor, health supervisor and director." See *Fifty Years: Serving Humanity through Education, Methodist-Kahler School of Nursing, 1918-1968* (1968): 26. Xeroxed copy, Mayo Historical Unit, M-K archives.

64 Audrey Snyder and Arlene Keeling, "'Contrary to Approved Methods of Practice': Massage Therapy, Polio, and Nursing, 1900-1945" (unpublished manuscript).

65 Strand, *A Century of Caring,* 64.

66 Ibid.

67 St. Mary's Hospital, *News Bulletin,* 5, 10 (October 1946):1. See also: Dunphy, "The Steel Cocoon," 4-5.

68 Ibid., 1.

69 Whelan, *The Sister's Story, Part 2,* 137.

70 Sister Mary Brigh Cassidy, "Minutes of the Meeting of the Coordination Committee St. Mary's Hospital" (August 9, 1949): 1. Mayo Historical Unit, Polio File.

71 Sister Mary Brigh Cassidy, "Minutes of the Meeting of Hospital Coordinating Committee St. Mary's Hospital" (September 5, 1949): 1. Mayo Historical Unit, Polio File.

72 "Urgent Appeal Goes Out For Nurses to Ease Polio Load at St. Mary's," (September 9, 1949). Mayo Historical Unit. Saint Marys archives.

73 Sister Mary Brigh, "Minutes of the Meeting of Hospital Coordinating Committee, St. Mary's Hospital" (November 7, 1949).

74 Whelan, *The Sister's Story Part 2,* 140.

75 Eleanor C. Lambertson, *Nursing Team Organization and Functioning: Results of a Study of the Division of Nursing Education, Teachers College, Columbia University,* (New York: Bureau of Publications, Teachers College, Columbia University, 1953). See also Sister M. Amadeus Klein, "A Study to Determine the Opinions of Selected Licensed Practical Nurses Concerning Factors which Affect Work Performance" (dissertation,

Washington D.C.: Catholic University of America, June 1962): 1-136, quote p. 3.

[76] Whelan, *The Sister's Story Part 2*, 88.

[77] Sister Amadeus Klein, Reprint (1977). In 1974, the Rochester School of Practical Nursing and Homemakers Program was accredited by the National League for Nursing (NLN).

[78] "The Rochester School for Practical Nurses and Homemakers Brochure," (1947): 1-4.

[79] "The Rochester School for Practical Nurses and Homemakers Begins," *St. Mary's News Bulletin* (January, 1948): 1.

[80] Whelan, *The Sisters' Story, Part 2*, 102.

[81] Ibid. See also Mayo Nursing Care Model: Individualizing Care.

[82] Sister Antoine Murphy, interview by Arlene Keeling, 2012. Transcript.

[83] Clark Nelson, *Mayo Roots: Profiling the Origins of Mayo Clinic* (Rochester: Mayo Foundation for Medical Education and Research,* 1990).

[84] A.P. Naef, "The Mid-Century Revolution in Thoracic and Cardiovascular Surgery: Part 2," *Interactive Cardiovascular and Thoracic Surgery,* 2 (2003): 431-449.

[85] Denton A. Cooley, "In Memoriam—John W. Kirklin, M.D., 1917-2004," Circulation (2004).

[86] *Fifty Years: Serving Humanity through Education, Methodist-Kahler School of Nursing, 1918-1968* (1968): 1-31.

[87] Ibid.

[88] Methodist-Kahler Alumae, interview by Arlene Keeling, May 29, 2012.

[89] Faye Abdellah and E. Josephine Starchan, "Progressive Patient Care," *American Journal of Nursing*, 59, 5 (May, 1959): 549-55. "In 1957, Faye Abdellah and her colleague Josephine Starchan, both nurses at Manchester

Memorial Hospital in Connecticut, proposed a system of Progressive Patient Care, defining it as the 'organization of facilities, services and staff around the medical and nursing needs of the patients.'" For further reading on this subject, see Arlene Keeling, Chapter 5, "Expanding Nurses' Scope of Practice," *Nursing and the Privilege of Prescription, 1893-2000"* (Columbus, Ohio: Ohio State University Press, 2007).

[90] Abdellah and Starchan, "Progressive Patient Care," 549-55.

[91] Ibid.

[92] For more reading on the history of intensive care, see Julie Fairman and Joan Lynaugh, *Critical Care Nursing: A History* (Philadelphia: University of Pennsylvania Press, 1998). See also Joan Lynaugh and Julie Fairman, "New Nurses, New Spaces: A Preview of the AACN History Survey," *American Journal of Critical Care* 1, 1 (1992): 19-24.

[93] Ibid. See also Keeling, Chapter 5 in *Nursing and the Privilege of Prescription*. Hill Burton funds made possible the rapid growth of hospitals throughout the United States at this time.

[94] Whelan, *The Sisters' Story, Part 2*, 162.

[95] Nelson, *Mayo Roots,* 334-335.

[96] "Special Hospital Unit Again Points UP Local Medical Work's 'Interdependence,'" *Mayovox* (January 11, 1958): 2.

[97] Eelico Wijdicks, Wendy Worden, Anne Miers, and David Piegras, "The Early Days of the Neurosciences Intensive Care Unit," Historical Vignette, *Mayo Clinic Proceedings,* 86, 9 (September 2011): 903-906.

[98] Sister Mary Brigh and Sister Mary Amadeus Klein, "Intensive Care: Effective Care," Hospital Progress (December, 1958): 1-4.

Reprint: Rochester. Mayo Historical Unit, Saint Marys School of Nursing archives. See also Wijdicks, Worden, Miers, and Piepofas, "The Early Days of the Neurosciences Intensive Care Unit," 903-906.

[99] Ibid.

[100] Madelyne Sturdavant, "Intensive Nursing Service in Circular and Rectangular Units Compared," *Journal of the American Hospital Association* (July 16, 1960). Reprint: Rochester. Mayo Historical Unit.

[101] Victor Cohn, "Rochester to Test Hospital-in-Round," *Minneapolis Tribune* (n.d.). Reprint: Rochester. Mayo Historical Unit.

[102] "Circular Hospital Concept 'Proves Out' at Methodist," *Mayovox* (June 11, 1960). Reprint: Rochester. Mayo Historical Unit.

[103] John L. Graner, *A History of the Department of Internal Medicine at the Mayo Clinic* (Rochester: The Mayo Foundation for Medical Education and Research, 2002): 263.

[104] Lawrence E. Meltzer, Rose Pinneo, and Rodderick Kitchell, *Intensive Coronary Care: A Manual for Nurses* (Philadelphia: Presbyterian Hospital, 1965): Preface.

[105] Lawrence E. Meltzer and J. Roderick Kitchell, Grant Proposal NU00096-01. Copy in The University of Virginia, Eleanor Crowder Bjoring Center for Nursing Historical Inquiry, Pinneo Collection.

[106] Mayo Foundation for Medical Education and Research, "First FDA-Approved Total Hip Replacement," https://www.mayoclinic.org/tradition-heritage/first-total-hip-replacement.html (accessed November 6, 2012).

[107] Elwood Wilkins, C.R.N.A., "Mayo Trained and Battle Tested," Mayo School of Health Sciences, *Connections* (Fall 2009), http://www.mayo.edu/mayo-edu-docs/alumni-

documents/mc4192-1109.pdf (accessed December 28, 2012).

[108] Jennifer Rosenberg, "Vietnam War Timeline," http://history1900s.about.com/od/vietnamwar/a/vietnamtimeline.htm. (accessed December 28, 2012).

[109] Wilkins, "Mayo Trained and Battle Tested."

[110] Adam Holland, personal communication to Arlene Keeling, "Military Nurses, Mayo Clinic."

[111] "History of the Methodist-Kahler School of Nursing, 1918-1968 " (circa 1968): 23. Xeroxed copy, Mayo Historical Unit, Methodist-Kahler archives.

[112] *Nursing Historical Highlights* (Rochester: Mayo Foundation for Medical Education and Research, 2012).

[113] Eleanor Smith, "Letter to Alumnae, Methodist-Kahler School of Nursing" (May 12, 1970): 1-2; quote p. 2. Smith was a 1936 Methodist-Kahler School of Nursing graduate.

[114] Sister Mary Brigh Cassidy, "Reminiscing Marks Nursing School Closing," *Rochester Post Bulletin* (Saturday, May 23, 1970).

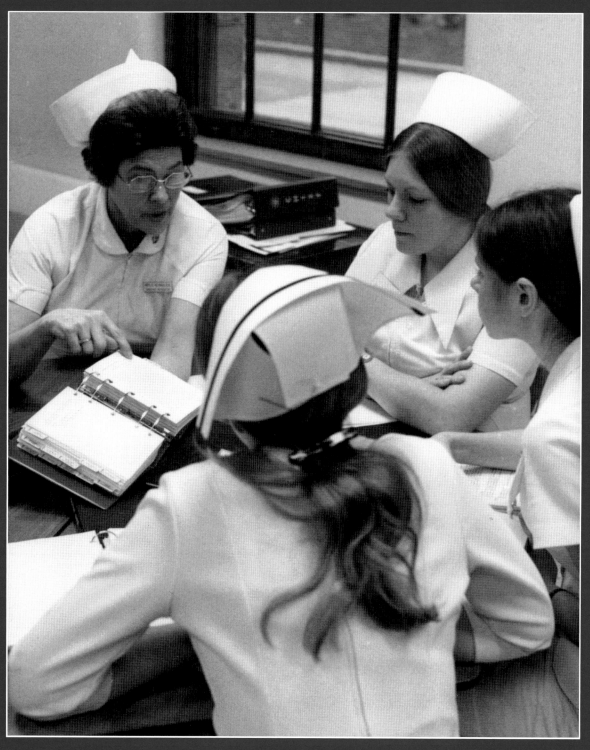

After the close of the hospital-based nursing schools, it became even more important to communicate Mayo's values and methods through on-the-job interactions.

CHAPTER IV

SPECIALIZATION & INTEGRATION

1971-1991

Before, during, and after her service as administrator of Saint Marys Hospital, Sister Generose Gervais focused on commitment to the patient.

During the 1970s, the hospitals in Rochester felt the impact of closing the Saint Marys and Methodist-Kahler Schools of Nursing. In particular, the lack of the two diploma programs affected the source of nurse staffing. Rather than coming to Rochester for their education and then staying on at Mayo-affiliated hospitals or at Mayo Clinic, nurses would now come to Mayo as graduates of other programs—some with baccalaureate credentials in nursing, some with associate degrees, and others as licensed practical nurses. Mayo values and Mayo methods would now have to be learned on the job and as a result, both Saint Marys Hospital and Rochester Methodist Hospital would need a nurse orientation program to prepare newly hired nurses to meet the needs of Mayo patients. That said, the hospitals affiliated with Mayo Clinic were well staffed with physicians, nurses, and other personnel already thoroughly rooted in the Mayo culture and familiar with Mayo methods to teach the new staff. The legacy would endure.

At Saint Marys, the legacy continued under new leadership; Sister Generose Gervais assumed the role of hospital administrator when Sister Mary Brigh Cassidy retired after twenty-two years in the position.[1] Sister Generose was perfect for the task. Her education in administration plus her years as assistant administrator to Sister Mary Brigh provided the experience and knowledge she needed to make a seamless transition. She would be a dynamic leader, with her commitment to "vision, faith, and hope to see what things can and must become."[2]

Shortages and Specialization

The decades of the 1970s and 1980s brought both challenges and changes to nursing in Rochester. Among these were a nursing shortage and an increasing emphasis on specialization—both of which paralleled national trends. Other changes included the establishment of numerous intensive care units—one for almost every subspecialty in medicine and surgery—accompanied, in 1971, by the initiation of a critical care nursing education program.

The development of the clinical nurse specialist role paralleled these initiatives. The 1970s ushered in a period of rapid growth and development in advanced practice nursing throughout the United States. By 1974, the American Nurses Association's Congress of Nursing Practice published educational standards for the clinical nurse specialist role and attempted to define the expanding scope of nursing practice.[3] Nurse administrators throughout the country soon began to hire for the role, developing job descriptions in

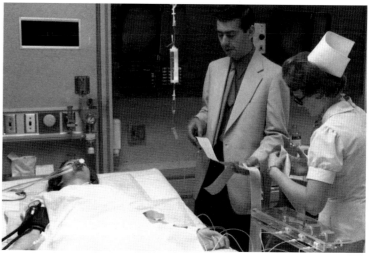

The rise of technology and specialization led to new opportunities for professional development in nursing, such as this photo of cardiac treatment in the intensive care unit.

collaboration with the newly educated clinical nurse specialists. Within a decade, the clinical nurse specialist had moved into mainstream nursing, and Mayo Clinic nurse leaders were on board. The new role proved beneficial for nurses and patients alike; it integrated a high level of nursing expertise, as well as practical, theoretical, and research-based competencies, ensuring that these experts not only gave direct patient care, but also taught staff nurses and provided them with consultation on complicated patient issues.[4]

The acceptance of the clinical nurse specialist role within the profession exemplified the growing recognition of specialty and subspecialty medical and nursing practice throughout the nation. At Mayo Clinic, the concept of specialty practice was not new. In Rochester, the original Mayo doctors and their colleagues each had areas of specialization, while nurses cared for patients with a

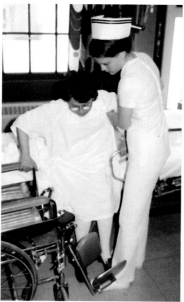

In the 1970s, the pantsuit became an accepted option for the nursing uniform.

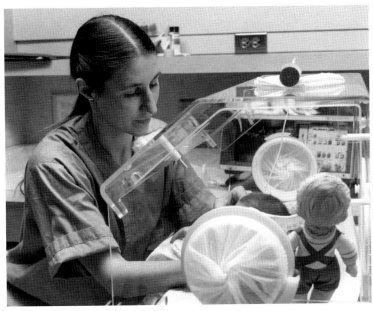
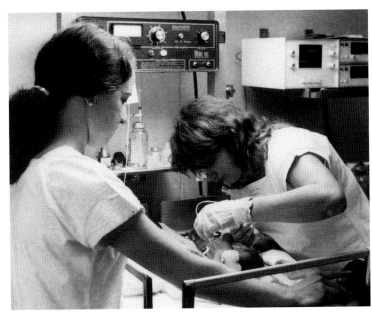

Mayo nurses effectively balanced a caring spirit with technical proficiency in the neonatal intensive care unit.

variety of conditions on general medical-surgical wards. By the 1920s, nurses had also begun to specialize according to the areas in which they worked. For nurses, most of their specialty training was done on the job or in post-diploma courses, like those for nurse anesthetists. For example, at Saint Marys in the mid-twentieth century, the emphasis on surgical care led to a certification program in operating room nursing.[5] By the late 1960s, with the growth of medical and surgical specialties and the rise of intensive care units, nurses' work became even more specialized.

In Rochester, the newborn intensive care unit (NICU) opened in 1972 on the sixth floor of the Francis Building at Saint Marys Hospital; nurses became experts in the care of premature infants as well as seriously ill newborns and infants up to the age of one year.[6] There, under the direction of Nursing Coordinator Mary Pregler, R.N., nurses provided high-tech care

COMMITMENT

"Our greatest challenge is a personal one. It is the challenge of commitment. Commitment to the welfare of the patient..."

SISTER GENEROSE GERVAIS

to help infants survive the first critical months of life.[7] To do so, the nurses had to have expert knowledge and specific skills in neonatal nursing.

With the growth of specialty practice, the organization and supervision of nursing was becoming increasingly complicated. At the same time that nurses in specialty areas were advocating for decentralized orientation and continuing education, nursing administrators were attempting to centralize various aspects of support, including such functions as infection control and intravenous therapy.[8] At Mayo Clinic, a centralized approach for overall nurse staffing was developed to assure that patient needs could be addressed across all units in the hospital. Staff nurses would float among the various nursing units, depending upon patient needs. The situation was challenging and would become more so as the profession introduced innovative approaches to patient care.

91

Innovation: Primary Nursing

One of the first challenges that nursing leaders at Saint Marys and Rochester Methodist Hospitals faced in the early 1970s was the introduction of Primary Nursing. The novel approach to patient-centered care contrasted to team nursing, the conventional method of providing nursing care in many hospitals at the time.

In 1973, Rochester Methodist Hospital Stations 42, 63, and the Alcoholism Treatment Unit all adopted Primary Nursing.[9] Under the new model of care, a primary nurse was assigned to each patient shortly after admission. The primary nurse was to have responsibility and authority for the nursing care that patients received throughout their hospital stay.[10] The new model allowed for a decentralization of decision making, giving the primary nurse total responsibility for the plan and the coordination of care, from the admission to the dismissal of the patient.[11] The primary nurse would instruct a secondary nurse, who was assigned to a patient for a specific shift, on the nursing interventions or plan of care that was to be followed in the primary nurse's absence. The primary nurse made rounds with the patient's doctor, promoting communication and collaboration to address patients' needs. This was a change in procedure; previously, only the head nurse was expected to communicate with physicians.

In theory, Primary Nursing was an excellent idea. In reality, it was difficult to implement, as it required a significant level of coordination to assure that a registered nurse was assigned to each patient for the entire length of stay in order to coordinate care. At Saint Marys and Rochester Methodist Hospitals (and in hospitals throughout the nation), the introduction of the new model was further complicated by a nursing shortage.

Left: Helen Jameson, R.N., became director of nursing service at Rochester Methodist Hospital in 1975. Her many contributions included alignment of nursing service and education. Right: Sister Jean Keniry, R.N., became director of nursing service at Saint Marys Hospital in 1978, bringing to the role a strong academic, clinical, and professional experience.

Transformational Leadership

It was into this setting that Helen Jameson, R.N., stepped when she accepted the position of director of nursing services at Rochester Methodist Hospital in 1975. Responding to the nursing shortage was her first challenge. Like other nursing administrators throughout the country, she particularly needed nurses to staff the new intensive care units. Her second challenge was that of uniting an increasingly decentralized and specialized nursing staff while simultaneously working within a hierarchical, central nursing administrative structure.

Helen Jameson had the necessary skills to address these challenges. She had both a bachelor's and a master's degree in nursing administration from the University of Minnesota and had been the director of patient care services at Mt. Sinai Hospital in Minneapolis from 1963 to 1975. Moreover, at Rochester Methodist Hospital, she had a supportive staff including, in particular, Associate Director Sharon Tennis, R.N., who had come to Rochester in 1965 as the first assistant instructor at Methodist-Kahler School of Nursing to have a bachelor of science in nursing degree.[12] With the help of her staff, using her

own creative leadership talents and working long hours, Helen Jameson was able to launch numerous initiatives.[13] Among these included: a head nurse development program; the formation of a Joint Committee on Nursing Service and Nursing Education; a nursing program in dermatology; a procedure for discharge planning; a collaborative program with the University of Minnesota to facilitate master's education in nursing; the development of a Nursing Education Department; and the establishment of Family-Centered Maternity Care at Rochester Methodist Hospital. Later in her career, in recognition of these achievements, the University of Minnesota honored her as one of its 100 Distinguished Alumni.[14]

Among the most significant of the Jameson-era's initiatives was the formation of the Joint Committee on Nursing Service and Nursing Education in 1975. The purpose of the committee was to provide the means for formal and consistent communication between nursing service and nursing education with a primary objective of facilitating the coordination of clinical facilities with nursing student experiences. As Helen Jameson remarked, "Nursing Service and Nursing Education need to work together...the students contribute to an environment of learning and inquiry. At the same time the hospital...is able to provide clinical experiences to help in preparing good graduates."[15] Bringing together nurse leaders from the Rochester hospitals, Public Health Department, along with faculty in the schools of nursing was critical to achieving a coordinated effort. Since 1936, the College of Saint Teresa had partnered with Saint Marys Hospital for a bachelor's of science in nursing clinical instruction; Rochester Area Vocational and Technical School was already

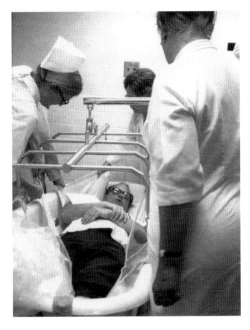

Jane Daniels, R.N. (left), demonstrated the use of a specially designed lift to assist patients who received dermatological treatment.

providing education for nursing assistants; and in 1976, Rochester Methodist Hospital would begin its affiliation with the nursing program of Luther College in effort to support and encourage nursing preparation at the baccalaureate level.[16]

In 1975, under Helen Jameson's leadership, Rochester Methodist Hospital also began its Dermatologic Nursing Program, an educational program designed to develop registered nurses' expertise in the specialty. Dermatology Nurse Specialist Jane Daniels, R.N., served as director and instructor for the program, working closely with Harold Perry, M.D., Mayo Clinic consultant in dermatology and medical coordinator of the program. The one-week program, funded by the National Program for Dermatology, covered a wide range of information, including anatomy and physiology, psychological effects of skin disease, presentation of dermatologic conditions, nursing procedures, dermatology pharmacology, and ultraviolet light therapy. The course included classroom demonstrations as well as clinical practice on one of the nursing areas, Station 8-2. As had been true since the inception of dermatology as a specialty at Mayo Clinic, nursing care was central to treatment for patients with skin disorders.[17] Now teaching other nurses what they had learned from their experience at Mayo would become central to the dermatology nurses' role.

Not only were nurses teaching other nurses, they were also focusing on teaching patients. In March 1976, Rochester Methodist Hospital's employee newsletter, *Inside Story,* highlighted nursing's efforts in patient education in other areas besides dermatology, noting that the nurses in pediatrics had "Discharge Planning under way."[18] The expanded discharge educational program, begun on nursing

Stations 6-1 and 6-2, included home management for patients recovering from hip replacement surgery. Under the leadership of Nursing Education Specialist Cathy Torkelson, R.N., the program gave patients the knowledge and skills they needed to manage their medical conditions after hospital discharge. In addition, nurses arranged for public health nurse follow-up. The program was needed; since Mark Coventry, M.D., completed the first Food and Drug Administration-approved hip replacement at Mayo Clinic in 1969, the number of orthopedic surgeries at Mayo had increased exponentially (see Chapter 3).[19]

Focus on Nursing Education
One of the major changes in continuing education for nurses at Rochester Methodist Hospital in 1976 was the formation of the new Division of Nursing Education to meet nurses' learning needs. The newly formed division would help create consistency throughout the hospital by placing educators on each unit in staff positions. Each would have additional education in teaching clinical and leadership skills that could be utilized by more than one unit and would have enough mobility to reach greater numbers of staff. However, in order "to zero in on the unit level," clinical educators would be assigned to specific units, working closely with the coordinator and head nurse.[20] Ann Umhoeffler, R.N., was the first of six clinical educators to be hired for the Division of Nursing Education. Coming to Rochester with

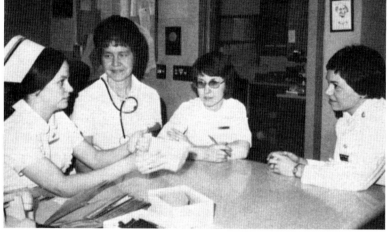

Discharge planning became increasingly important with the availability of specialized procedures such as total hip replacement.
From left: Donna Jones, R.N., met with nursing colleagues to discuss postoperative strategy for orthopedic patients.

a master's of science degree in psych-mental health nursing from the University of Minnesota, she exemplified the move towards requiring higher education for specialty practice within the profession.[21]

Clearly, preparing nurses to be experts in advanced practice (with advanced courses in pathophysiology and pharmacology at the master's level as well as in nursing theory, health promotion, nursing research, and other courses in their specialty) was becoming increasingly important. On June 4, 1976, Mayo Clinic announced that the University of Minnesota had selected Rochester as a location for a new external degree program for a master's in nursing. The advanced educational opportunity was met with excitement and enthusiastic support. The program made it easier for Mayo nurses to obtain a master's degree—a requirement for becoming a clinical nurse specialist—without having to leave their jobs to do so.[22] The decision was a good one; that year, leaders at Saint Marys Hospital expressed their commitment to the value of the clinical nurse specialist role, planning to hire these advanced practice nurses.

Family-Centered Maternity Care
In the spring of 1977, after years of planning, renovation, and under the leadership of Barbara Moulton, R.N., the obstetrics unit relocated from Saint Marys Hospital to the third and fourth floors of Rochester

Methodist Hospital. The new delivery area, located on the third floor, featured state-of-the-art equipment and technology, including a blanket and solution warmer, radiant heating units in the recovery room, and fetal monitors in each room. Between the delivery rooms was a pediatrician's area with neonatal intensive care cribs, as well as special lighting and oxygen outlets, all strategically placed to provide emergency resuscitation should the newborn require it.[23] On the fourth floor were eighteen postpartum beds and twenty-five bassinets.

Pediatrics remained at Saint Marys. Thus, premature and critically ill infants born at Rochester Methodist Hospital would be transferred "in specialized ultra-modern portable life-support" carriers to Saint Marys Hospital where they would be admitted to the neonatal intensive care facilities.[24]

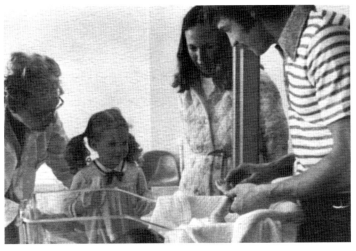

Nurses at Rochester Methodist Hospital helped develop programs to involve older children with their newborn siblings—a principle in family-centered care.

According to newspaper accounts about the open house that took place before the move to Rochester Methodist Hospital, nurses in the new unit would emphasize family-centered maternity care, combining the most modern physical facilities and the best professional services, with a strong awareness of the needs of the patient as an individual and as a member of a family. In fact, the new unit incorporated such home influences as rocking chairs in each of the rooms and in the nursery.[25] In the new setting, babies could be taken out of the nursery in the mothers' rooms during the day, as much or as little as the mothers wanted. To provide coordination of care, one nurse would be assigned to each mother and her baby.[26] In keeping with family-

centered care, but consistent with restrictions on visiting newborns typical of this era, older brothers and sisters could visit by peering through glass separating a children's room from the mother's day room.[27]

In the new family-centered maternity unit, preparing mothers for the childbirth experience and following them after delivery was part of the nurse's role. Prenatal classes, including tours of the facilities, were initiated in late March, a few weeks prior to the unit's opening. Later, the nurse assigned to the mother during hospitalization would be available by telephone to answer questions the mother might have after she returned home with her newborn. Indeed, communication with new mothers would be an essential component of quality patient care.

Growth of Specialties

While family-centered maternity care was being implemented at Rochester Methodist Hospital, specialty practice continued to grow within the institution. Established earlier, intensive care, coronary care, cardiac surgery, and dermatology all continued to develop, as did psychiatry and pediatrics. In addition, the renal dialysis and transplant units were evolving. In these specialized units, highly trained nurses gave dialysis treatments to patients to filter their blood, monitoring them minute by minute for complications and intervening as necessary. For patients whose kidney failure was extreme, the nurses prepared them for transplant.[28]

As health care grew more complex, nurses remained focused on communication, collaboration, and teamwork. From left: Mary Trenda, R.N., and Peggy Kuiper, R.N., discussed a patient's plan of care.

Growth in specialty practice once again necessitated hospital expansion and on September 30, 1980, Saint Marys Hospital opened its largest addition to date, the Mary Brigh Building a structure that housed new intensive care beds, surgical suites, radiology facilities, and space for future expansion.[29] Growth in specialty practice also required the continued development of nursing expertise in specific clinical areas and in 1981, Rochester Methodist Hospital hired master's-prepared Diane Block, R.N., as its first clinical specialist for obstetrics, gynecology, and pediatrics. Employing a clinical nurse specialist reflected the profession's, as well as Rochester's growing acceptance of the new role. In return, the nurse specialist added a new level of clinical expertise. According to a report from the Task Force on Nursing Practice in Hospitals, clinical specialists added a "dimension of nursing care that would otherwise not be available to patients and their families."[30] Over the remainder of the twentieth century, the clinical nurse specialist role would continue to evolve.

Part of that role would be to serve as a resource to staff nurses who were seeing increasing numbers of patients with complicated medical conditions and complex care needs.

Staffing to Patients' Needs

Concurrent with the growth of specialty practice and increasing national concerns about the cost of health care in the 1980s, clinical directors and unit head nurses began to examine the issue of cost containment. During the 1980s, constraints imposed by diagnosis related groups (DRGs), the newly created prospective payment system designed to limit the share of hospital revenues derived from the Medicare program budget, revolutionized medical financing and had a widespread impact on hospitals across the nation.[31] As a result, many organizations began to staff hospitals by patient volume and DRGs. At Mayo Clinic, however, staffing to patient workload continued to be the guiding principle, and Rochester Methodist and Saint Marys Hospital nursing supervisors staffed the hospital to meet the patients' needs for nursing care.[32]

In Mayo's staffing-to-workload approach, staff nurses assessed patient care needs using a research-based patient classification system that assigned each patient a level of acuity reflecting the patient's need for nursing care. Patient care needs could include medication preparation and management, cardiovascular and other nurse assessments, discharge planning, needs related to activities of daily living, and such treatments as complicated wound dressings. For example, patients who needed close observation, multiple medications through intravenous lines, and much teaching prior to discharge would require more care hours than a patient who had a simple surgical procedure and same day discharge.

Based on the nursing unit's total workload for all patients, a staffing recommendation matrix for each unit was created, identifying the numbers of registered nurses, licensed practical nurses and patient care assistants required to care for the patients. Using the recommended number of staff ensured that the right number of nurses and assistants were available to meet patient needs from shift to shift.

Based on the Mayo Clinic value of the primacy of the patient, staffing to meet patients' needs was be the foundation on which hiring decisions about nursing personnel were made—even when there was a hiring freeze in other aspects of the organization. Indeed, staffing to patients' needs was foundational to quality patient care at Mayo Clinic.[33] The use of three alternatives: 1) an internal float pool, 2) unit staff working on other patient care units, and 3) staff taking voluntary extra shifts or voluntary days off depending on staffing needs, as well as a policy of not employing outside travel or agency nurses, became hallmarks of nurse staffing in Rochester. Using only Mayo nurses would ensure that Mayo Clinic could provide the highest quality of patient care.

From left: Sister June Kaiser, representing Saint Marys Hospital; W. Eugene Mayberry, M.D., representing Mayo Clinic; and George Groves, representing Rochester Methodist Hospital, signed an agreement on May 28, 1986, that integrated the three organizations into a single "trusteeship for health."

Magnet Recognition for Nursing

In 1983, after a national research study, the American Academy of Nursing named Rochester Methodist hospital a Magnet Hospital and a model of nursing practice for its success in attracting and retaining nurses. Magnet designation recognizes "nursing input into policies affecting practice, opportunities to practice the profession of nursing and provision for professional growth for nurses."[34] The landmark study was the forerunner to the Magnet Recognition Program developed by the American Nurses Credentialing Center in 1990. In 1997,

Mayo Hospitals in Rochester were the fifth in the nation to be designated under the new program. Over the next 14 years, that designation would be repeated in 2002, 2007, and 2011.[35]

"When the Integration Came Along"[36]

For years, administrators of the hospitals affiliated with Mayo Clinic had been planning to unite their services to standardize practice and avoid duplication of services, and on March 6, 1986, leaders representing Saint Marys Hospital, Mayo Clinic, and Rochester Methodist Hospital signed an integration agreement to begin the process. On May 28, 1986, the terms were fulfilled and Sister June Kaiser of Saint Marys Hospital, W. Eugene Mayberry, M.D., of Mayo Clinic, and George Groves of Rochester Methodist Hospital signed the historic agreement, joining the two hospitals and Mayo Clinic into a single united governing structure.[37] The goal was to redefine and formalize the relationship structure between these long-time partners.

Signing an agreement to integrate was the easy part. With it came the complicated matter of translating policy into a working environment that now included 14,000 men and women, including nurses, physicians and surgeons, nursing assistants, finance officers, desk personnel, and maintenance people while maintaining everyone's dignity, ambitions, and concerns that needed to be recognized and addressed.[38] That process, done with the utmost respect for personnel,

Representing Mayo's leadership and strengthening bonds with hospital colleagues, Drs. Robert Waller (left) and W. Eugene Mayberry greeted Patricia Bremer, R.N. (second from right) and Joyce Overman Dube, R.N. (right) of Rochester Methodist Hospital soon after it joined with Mayo Clinic and Saint Marys Hospital in 1986.

the hospital names, and continuity of patient care, would take time. It would also require participation from the entire staff if it were to be accomplished. Participation was forthcoming; with the skills, attitudes, and caring spirit of the Mayo staff, it was sure to succeed.[39]

One of the major challenges to integration would be that of uniting the nursing services of Saint Marys Hospital and Rochester Methodist Hospital. In 1986, Director of Nursing Support Services Sharon Tennis, R.N., was directly involved in the process, along with other nurse leaders.[40] Over the next years, teams of nurses from both hospitals formed work groups to tackle areas for integration, including nurse recruitment and hiring, scheduling and staffing policies, and nursing practice policies and procedures. In addition, these teams addressed issues related to nursing culture and leadership roles. As with any major change, uniting two large nursing departments into one integrated entity was not easy and the process did not move quickly. Each of the departments had a long and proud history of nursing care.

Clearly, Saint Marys and Rochester Methodist Hospitals were distinct. Each had its own culture. Saint Marys' culture was based on the precepts of the Roman Catholic Church and was the first hospital in Rochester to open in collaboration with Dr. W.W. Mayo. Rochester Methodist Hospital also had a unique identity and culture. Since the inception of the Colonial Training School in 1918, and its subsequent renaming as the Kahler School of Nursing and later Methodist-Kahler, its nursing alumnae had a unique identity as "Kahlerites."[41] Since 1954, when the hospital formed as a nonprofit, their culture had been based on Methodist values.

While there was ongoing cooperation between the two schools and their leaders, as well as between the two hospitals and their directors, there was also some sibling rivalry at the grassroots level. Students and faculty in each school considered their own education and nursing practices best. Now, in spite of the fact that both schools had been closed for sixteen years, uniting the nurses in the two hospitals under a common governing structure would not be easy. Unifying the nursing resource section into one that would serve both hospitals was an early goal and Sharon Tennis, R.N., became director of nursing resources for both hospitals in 1990. The new nursing resource section included nursing workload measurement, budget planning, nurse recruitment/hiring, nurse scheduling and staffing, nurse float staffs, and nursing supervisors. It would provide a common infrastructure to support future practice integration.

Sharon Tennis worked constantly to understand the different cultures related to nursing resources and to bring the two nursing services together, meeting frequently with head nurses from both hospitals as well as with nursing resource staff. Reflecting on the situation, she recalled, "We did not yet have a Department of Nursing and few systems were integrated. It was difficult work and yet invigorating as we began to create something new...Overall, it was one of my most satisfying experiences."[42]

Beyond Rochester, Minnesota

The integration work continued as Mayo Clinic expanded. Mayo Clinic and Rochester, Minnesota, had been synonymous for almost a century, but in the 1980s, after years of planning, that changed when Mayo's leaders decided to apply the same basic system of patient care in both Florida and Arizona.[43] Mayo Clinic in Florida was built first, and on May 11, 1985, six dignitaries turned shovelfuls of dirt, marking the groundbreaking for Mayo's $24 million facility in the city of Jacksonville. According to one report, "it was a garden party, complete with a blue and white striped canopy tent," in the middle of nowhere—a nowhere that Jacksonville's leaders predicted would soon become the somewhere of medical care in the southeast.[44] The new clinic, built on 140 acres of pine and brush forest donated by J.E. Davis, opened in the fall of 1986 with a staff of 30 physicians and 120 support personnel, including nurses for each specialty.[45]

In Jacksonville, Mayo Clinic would provide adult outpatient specialty care, focusing on the areas of cardiology, nephrology, gastroenterology, and later, solid organ transplant. The Jacksonville area already had several acute care hospitals for inpatient services, so the new clinic provided outpatient diagnostic and treatment services only.[46] Patients who needed hospitalization were admitted to local hospitals, including St. Luke's Hospital, the oldest hospital in Florida and one with an excellent reputation for nursing care.[47] Working with Mayo physicians, St. Luke's nurses began to adopt Mayo values; from the start it was evident to them that the needs of the patient came first.[48]

In its first expansion outside of Minnesota, Mayo Clinic opened a facility in Jacksonville, Florida, in 1986.

Mayo Clinic opened a campus in Scottsdale, Arizona, in 1987. The Nature Trail and other features incorporate the beauty of the desert into the healing process.

Four of the original nurses from the opening of Mayo Clinic in Arizona are: (front left to right) Carol Ann Attwood, R.N., Linda Schwartz, R.N., (back left to right) Amy Ganske, R.N., and Shannon Glasshof, R.N.

In 1987, Mayo Clinic opened its new facility in Scottsdale, Arizona. Like Mayo Clinic in Florida, the adult specialty clinic, with its 120 examination rooms, onsite lab testing and analysis, diagnostic imaging, two outpatient operating rooms, advanced satellite telecommunication, pharmacy, and a patient education library, was an outpatient facility, providing services in the specialties of neurology, cardiology, dermatology, and oncology. Patients requiring hospitalization were admitted to the nearby Scottsdale Memorial North Hospital (later called Scottsdale Healthcare Shea or Shea Medical Center).

When Mayo Clinic opened in Arizona, it had a staff of 42 physicians and 220 support personnel, 14 of whom were nurses.[49] Among these were Carol Ann Attwood, R.N., Amy Ganske, R.N., Linda Schwartz, R.N., Shannon Glasshof, R.N., and Nursing Director Jayne Baker, R.N. Working together amid unpacked boxes on opening day, these nurses shared resources, bartering and exchanging supplies to equip the new areas before all the equipment

arrived.[50] Adaptable, flexible, and willing to work as a team, the nurses were already expressing Mayo values.

From the start, nurses at Mayo Clinic in Arizona were part of the team, helping to design new spaces. Their views and ideas were taken seriously. From the oncology clinic nurses' perspective, it was important to have a light, open, and airy environment with large, comfortable recliners. In addition, snacks, puzzles, and reading material in the lobby would help comfort the patients who spent long days receiving chemotherapy. These changes were quickly incorporated into the oncology clinic environment. Meeting patients' needs was the priority.[51]

Achieving the Vision in Florida

While much was taking place out West, in October 1987, St. Luke's Hospital in Jacksonville, nine miles from Mayo's location, became a Mayo Clinic hospital.[52] The challenge now was to initiate Mayo methods and culture into the nursing department at St. Luke's. It would not be a simple matter. St. Luke's had a long history of its own and was staffed with numerous agency nurses—temporary traveling nurses. On the plus side, St. Luke's nurses, who had been working closely with Mayo physicians since Mayo Clinic had opened in Jacksonville, already felt that they were part of the Mayo Clinic team; they were well respected and their assessments of changes in patients' conditions were taken seriously and responded to promptly.[53]

To begin the process of introducing Mayo culture in St. Luke's, former Rochester Methodist Hospital Nursing Director Helen Jameson, R.N., traveled to Jacksonville in 1989 to consult on the nursing situation there. Surprised that St. Luke's was using eight to nine agency pools for nurse staffing, she worked with St. Luke's administrators to hire new full-time nursing staff. Collaborating with Vice President of Patient Services Nell Talbird, R.N., she also created Mayo's Nurse Exchange Program to include the first group of ten nurses from the Jacksonville area. The plan worked well; nurses from

*Japanese nurses visited
Mayo Clinic in Rochester.*

Rochester appreciated the opportunity to go south in the long Minnesota winters while Jacksonville nurses enjoyed a reprieve from Florida summers and a chance to work at the original and largest site of Mayo Clinic. The plan not only helped the staffing situation; it also facilitated the transfer of Mayo values and ways to the Florida location.[54]

Exchange Nursing with Japan
Integrating nursing among all Mayo sites was becoming increasingly challenging, and in 1989, the Mayo Clinic Board of Governors established the Mayo Center for Nursing under Director Anne Miers (Jones), R.N. Its purpose was to coordinate continuing nursing education, nursing research, and nursing practice among the various nursing settings, with the goal of pursuing excellence in nursing practice.[55] It was a significant step toward uniting nursing services in the two hospitals in Rochester, with membership on the executive committee including the Assistant Administrator for Nursing at Rochester Methodist Hospital, Sylvia Lufkin R.N., and the Assistant Administrator for Nursing at Saint Marys Hospital, Bruce Frederick R.N. However, it was not enough; it soon became evident that what was needed was a Department of Nursing, whose leader was accountable for nursing at the highest levels of decision making in Mayo Clinic.[56] That goal would be realized in 1991.

Exchange Nursing with Japan
Mayo Center for Nursing soon extended its influence across international borders, as Director Ann Miers (Jones), R.N., coordinated all international nurses' visits. Before this time, nurses at both Saint Marys Hospital and Rochester Methodist Hospital each coordinated these visits. Since 1966, Japanese nurses had visited Mayo Clinic in an exchange program facilitated by Haruo Okazaki, M.D, and his wife Bihkar Okazaki, R.N., as well as by Kiyomi Takekawa, R.N., a retired psychiatric nurse and her husband, Tom. Later, from 1995 until her retirement in 2007, Sandra Leinonen, R.N., coordinated the program. The objectives of the international exchange were to share Mayo Clinic's nursing mission, vision, and core values; to provide opportunities to observe and learn from nurses at all levels of practice within Mayo Clinic; and to provide nurse visitors with the opportunity to experience American culture.[57]

*Mayo Clinic nurses traveled to Japan, meeting
with colleagues and learning about the
Japanese health care system.*

Exchanging information about professional practice had been a core Mayo value since the nineteenth century when the Doctors Mayo welcomed both physicians and nurses from around the world. Now, the more formalized visitor exchange program was achieving its goals. Over the years since its inception, thousands of nurses from numerous countries had visited Mayo Clinic and in return, Mayo nurses had traveled to their countries. Even after 1991, when Mayo Center for Nursing ended, its mission would endure; Mayo Clinic nurses would continue to share their expertise around the world.

Nursing Research

The Nursing Research Committee, established in 1989 under the leadership of Associate Director of the Mayo Center for Nursing, Marilyn Stiles, R.N., and co-chaired by Dianne Axen, R.N., was an exciting new venture providing institutional recognition to previous research activities at Rochester Methodist and Saint Marys Hospitals.[58] Innovative as it was, it drew on a long history of nursing research at Mayo Clinic.

Jon Balgeman, R.N., and Maureen Bigelow, R.N., prepare equipment to research the impact of increased air pressure on intravenous fluid administration when a patient receives hyperbaric oxygen therapy.

transplant surgery. Still other nurses, like Sister Pantaleon Navratil, R.N., had helped physicians conduct clinical trials, assisting with the investigative procedures and collecting data. The new venture was also the result of groundwork at Rochester Methodist where the feasibility of establishing a nursing research program had been studied in 1978. At that time, two University of Minnesota Ph.D. nurse researchers concluded that there were sufficient resources within Rochester Methodist Hospital and the Mayo Medical Center to support a nursing research program. Now, the Nursing Research Committee united and organized scholarly efforts with a focus on defining and enhancing nursing research.

The research initiative reflected a growing movement within the nursing profession for the conduct of research to determine best practices for patient care (later, called evidenced-based practice) rather than basing nursing care solely on tradition. At Mayo Clinic, the Nursing Research Committee helped identify the best Mayo

A century earlier, Alice Magaw, R.N., and her nurse anesthesia colleagues had conducted descriptive studies of their work, keeping careful accounts of the number of inductions they did under the direction of the Doctors Mayo and publishing the results in reputable medical journals. Throughout the twentieth century, other nurses and their colleagues had written about innovative nursing methods at Mayo hospitals, such as the delivery of nursing care in the circular units. They had also described the care of patients after renal

practices rather than having nurses at each hospital rely on their own ways of doing things.

Shortly after its inception, the Nursing Research Committee focused its efforts on creating an environment to conduct nursing research.[59] They were successful. In 1991, the Board of Governors in Rochester allocated an annual budget for nursing research. The board also created research appointments for nurse investigators that were similar to other Mayo research appointments, provided nurse investigators with access to all Mayo research resources, and placed a nurse researcher on the Mayo Rochester Research Committee. All were significant steps in developing nursing research at Mayo Clinic.

With the purpose of supporting and integrating nursing research at Mayo Medical Center, the Nursing Research Committee would take nursing research to a new level.[60] Throughout the institution, an increasing number of nurses with master's and doctoral preparation used their skills in research methods and statistical analysis to design and implement clinical research projects and evaluate outcomes. Staff nurses identified research questions and participated in research projects. Within a year, in 1992, nurses at all levels would present their results at the First Annual Nursing Research Conference, sponsored by the Mayo Center for Nursing, the Kappa Mu Chapter of Sigma Theta Tau, and Winona State University. [61]

Integrating Nursing

In 1991, a milestone in Mayo Clinic nursing history occurred with the establishment of nursing as a clinical department. Departmental status recognized nursing as a discipline in alignment with physician-led clinical departments at Mayo. With the formation of the Department of Nursing, nursing services at Saint Marys and Rochester Methodist Hospitals began to standardize practice and procedures. Doreen Frusti, R.N., was appointed as the first chair of the Department of Nursing, charged with integrating hospital nursing across the two locations. She held a strong belief that if Mayo nursing was to be considered a professional discipline, all Mayo Clinic nurses should be members of their own department led by their own discipline. This meant a simple, direct reporting line, with nurses reporting

Doreen Frusti, R.N., was first chair of the Department of Nursing when it formed in 1991.

to nurses, giving nurses the full accountability and authority for nursing practice. She also understood the importance of ambulatory nurses reporting to the Department of Nursing. It was a goal that took years to achieve, but was well worth the effort. Integrating the ambulatory staff nurses under the department would symbolize the complete integration of Mayo nursing.

Doreen Frusti was well prepared to lead the new department through her clinical experience, passion for nursing, and educational preparation. She began her experience at Mayo Clinic as Summer III (externship for nursing students) in general surgery in 1969. She was hired as a staff nurse in 1970 and rose through the ranks as nurse manager and nurse administrator; she also obtained two master's degrees at Winona State University, one in psychology and counseling and the other in nursing administration. Being chair would be a challenging position, as the formation of the department was in and of itself a huge undertaking. Facing that challenge, she not only laid the foundation but also built the components of a professional nursing practice environment at Mayo Clinic.[62]

The newly formed Department of Nursing was immediately charged with making two nursing groups, from two very different hospitals, function as one.[63] Determined to succeed in fulfilling that charge, Doreen Frusti soon began a series of meetings with the staffs of each hospital and another series of monthly meetings with nurse managers. Her goal in these meetings was not only to have a presence with the staff and listen to their concerns but also to bring the best of each hospital's culture together.[64] Using this grassroots approach, she involved all nursing staff in strategic planning for the future.

Building on the philosophy statement developed earlier by the Mayo Center for Nursing Philosophy Task Force (formed in January 1990 and chaired by Phyllis Freeman, R.N.), Doreen Frusti led the new Department of Nursing in adopting its vision statement. It was both straightforward and idealistic: "To provide the best nursing care in the world."[65]

The new vision resonated with the philosophy first espoused by the Mayos and put into practice by the Sisters of Saint Francis more than a century earlier: care would be focused on the best interest of the patient. But, expanding on that philosophy, the vision statement also supported Mayo nurses' obligation to enhancing professionalism, continuing education, and participating in research.[66] Besides developing a vision statement, Doreen Frusti crafted a mission statement: "To deliver comprehensive nursing care of the highest standard to every Mayo patient through professional nursing practice,

LEARNING

"As a profession interested in enhancing patient care, we can never stop asking questions."

DIANNE AXEN, R.N.

education and research."[67] The mission included the caring and support of the patient and individuals important to the patient at any point along the health continuum. It also provided educational opportunities in clinical nursing and professional development for nursing staff, affiliated students and faculty, and regional, national, and international nursing colleagues.

In addition to the vision and mission statements, the department identified core values as the basis for nursing practice. These included the existence of a professional environment, professional nurse accountability for nursing care, and dedication to continuity of care— all values that would guide Mayo Clinic nursing in achieving its vision.[68] The values were reaffirmed in 2006 as the foundation of the Mayo Nursing Care Model. Defining principles of the values included patient-centered care, respect for the individual, a holistic approach to care, and patient advocacy. They also included the requirement that a registered nurse be assigned to each hospitalized patient and that a registered nurse be the coordinator of patient care. Commitment to collegial/interdisciplinary practice, shared decision making, education, research-based practice, and involvement in the local and professional community were also expected.

As chair of the newly formed Department of Nursing, Doreen Frusti wanted to advance Mayo nurses' professional practice by creating an environment in which nurses provided guidance to each other, were accountable to each other, set practices and procedures, shared in decisions that affected nursing practice, and collaborated with other members of the health care team. Nursing committees

Nurses focus on the unique needs of each patient in making clinical plans for the day.

Summer III Adrianne Wemmert and Clinical Coach Allison Meisheid, R.N., reviewed educational materials with a patient.

focusing on practice, education, and research, consistent with physician committees, ensured that standards were consistently applied in patient care. These committees, included the Nursing Education Committee, Nursing Clinical Practice Committee, Nursing Research Committee, and Mayo Nursing Council, empowered direct care nurses to be involved in decision making that affected nursing practice.[69]

Integrating the Summer III program

One of the initiatives the Department of Nursing undertook was the integration of the nurse tech and Summer III programs. The two original programs, providing a summer Mayo Clinical experience for student nurses selected from throughout the country, had originated at Rochester Methodist Hospital in 1966 and Saint Marys in 1967.

Now, under the leadership of Sharon Tennis, R.N, the highly competitive program offered to student nurses who were completing their third year of nursing education, would be known as the Mayo Summer III Nursing Program. Starting in June each year and lasting 10 weeks, Summer III offered its participants a chance to learn patient care in an area of their choosing. Paired with registered nurse coaches, the students experienced working at Mayo Clinic first hand, with in-depth understanding of the unique contributions that nurses made there.[70] The program, promoting a life-changing opportunity for professional growth, continued into the twenty-first century. In addition to its educational aspects, Summer III was a recruitment tool, inspiring exceptional students to consider a career at Mayo Clinic. It worked. Jasmine Ferguson, a Summer III student in 2012, explained the program's benefits:

"This summer was my first experience with critical care nursing and the learning curve was enormous! With the help of my coach and other nurses...they allowed me to have hands-on experience that connected the theoretical classroom knowledge with real-life situations! I felt as if I learned as much information and gained more skills than I had in a year of nursing school!"[71]

What Jasmine Ferguson and the Summer III students experienced was the realization of the vision that Doreen Frusti announced in 1991: Mayo Clinic nurses would provide the best nursing care in the world. It was a shared vision that united the past with the present. It was also a vision that would guide Mayo Clinic nursing through the challenges of the 1990s and into the twenty-first century.

ENDNOTES

1 "From One to Another," *Saint Marys News Bulletin,* 30, Special Issue (October 1971): 1-6. Sister Generose had been Associate Administrator under Sister Mary Brigh.

2 Ibid., 4.

3 Arlene Keeling and Jeri Bigbee, "The History of Advanced Practice Nursing in the United States," chap. 1 in *Advanced Practice Nursing: An Integrative Approach, 3rd ed., ed.* Ann Hamric, Judith Spross, and Charlene Hanson, 3-45 (St Louis: Elsevier Saunders, 2005).

4 Ann Hamric, "A Definition of Advanced Practice Nursing," chap. 3 in *Advanced Practice Nursing: An Integrative Approach, 3rd ed., ed.* Ann Hamric, Judith Spross, and Charlene Hanson, 89 (St Louis: Elsevier Saunders, 2005).

5 Mary Grobe, "Historical Overview: Common Themes, SMH and RMH" (June 1992): 1-17.

6 Kenneth McCracken, "St. Mary's Hospital Opens New Facility to Provide Intensive Care for Infants" (June 16, 1972). Reprint: Rochester. Mayo Historical Unit, Folder Saint Marys Hospital.

7 Ibid.

8 Grobe, "Historical Overview: Common Themes, SMH and RMH," 1-17.

9 "Primary Nursing Comes to RMH," The *Inside Story,* 13, 4 (January 26, 1973): 1-2, quote p.1.

10 Ibid., 1.

11 Ibid.

12 Sharon Tennis, interview by Arlene Keeling and Adam Holland, November 16, 2012. Transcript.

13 Helen Jameson, interview by Arlene Keeling and Adam Holland, 2012. Transcript.

14 Ibid. See also Jameson, curriculum vitae, Mayo Clinic; and Sharon Tennis, interview by Arlene Keeling and Adam Holland, November 16, 2012. Transcript.

15 Ibid.

16 *Nursing Historical Highlights* (Rochester: Mayo Foundation for Medical Education and Research, 2012).

17 "Dermatologic Nursing Program Draws From All Over U.S.," *RMH he Inside Story,* 15, 24 (August 15, 1975). Reprint: Rochester. Mayo Historical Unit.

18 "Nursing Services Very Active, Rapidly Growing: Discharge Planning Under Way," *RMH, The Inside Story,* 16, 13 (March 26, 1976): 1-2.

19 Ibid.

20 "Nursing Education: New Department for Special Needs," *RMH, The Inside Story,* 6, 1 (January 2, 1976): 1-3. Reprint: Rochester. Mayo Historical Unit.

21 "First of Six Clinical Educators Hired," *RMH, The Inside Story* (July 8, 1977). Mayo Historical Unit, Box 3: Nursing Education.

22 "U of M Masters in Nursing Coming to Rochester," *RMH, The Inside Story,* 16, 25 (June 18, 1976): 1-2.

23 "Family Centered Maternity Care," *RMH, The Inside Story,* 17, 8 (April 15, 1977): 6.

24 "New Obstetrics Unit" *RMH News* (Spring 1977): 2-3.

25 "Family Centered Maternity Care," 6.

26 Ibid.

27 Ibid.

28 "Kidney Dialysis and Transplant: Life's Second Chance," *RMH News* (Winter 1980).

29 "The Heritage and the Vision," *Caring '80* (1980): 8. Reprint: Rochester.

30 Ann Hamric and Judith Spross, *The Clinical Nurse Specialist in Theory and Practice, 2nd Ed.* (Philadelphia: WB Saunders, 1989): 5.

31 Wikipedia, "Diagnosis-related Group," http://en.wikipedia.org/wiki/Diagnosis-related_group (accessed December 29, 2012). See also Rick Mayes, "The Origins, Development and Passage of Medicare's Revolutionary Prospective Payment System," *Journal of the History of Medicine and Allied Sciences,* 62 (January 2007): 55.

32 Doreen Frusti, telephone interview by Arlene Keeling and Adam Holland, December 7, 2012. Transcript.

33 Ibid.

34 Helen Jameson, "100 Distinguished Alumni Award Nominee Information." Mayo Historical Unit.

35 "Academy Names 41 'Magnet' Hospitals Because of Their 'Demonstrated Success' in Attracting and Retaining Nurses," *American Nurse,* 2 (1983): 15.

36 Sister Genovese Gervais, personal communication with Arlene Keeling and Adam Holland, May 29, 2012.

37 Ibid., 185.

38 Ibid., 183.

39 Ibid., 185.

40 Sharon Tennis, interview by Arlene Keeling and Adam Holland, November 16, 2012. Transcript.

41 Carol Ann Wallace (M-K Class of 1955), Sandra Moore (M-K Class of 1966), Vaunette Alrick (M-K Class of 1968), and Suzanne Mattson (M-K Class of 1968), interview by Arlene Keeling and Adam Holland, May 29, 2012. See also, "Letters From the KSN Alumnae" *The Link* (1930-1970). The students and graduates referred to themselves as "Kahlerites."

42 Sharon Tennis, interview by Arlene Keeling

and Adam Holland, November 16, 2012. Transcript.

43 Holmes, *Dedicated to Excellence,* 182.

44 Evelyn Tovar, "Mayo Satellite Gets Dignified Welcome," *Florida Times-Union and Journal, Jacksonville* (May 11, 1985). Reprint: Rochester. Mayo Historical Unit, Mayo Clinic-Jacksonville archives.

45 Evelyn Tovar, "Mayo Clinic Will Adapt to Locale, Officials Say," *Florida Times-Union and Journal, Jacksonville* (Sunday August 26, 1984). Reprint: Rochester. Mayo Historical Unit, Mayo Clinic-Jacksonville archives.

46 "Our History: St. Luke's Hospital," brochure. Mayo Historical Unit, Mayo Clinic-Jacksonville archives.

47 Tovar, "Mayo Clinic Will Adapt."

48 Nursing Leaders from Mayo Clinic in Florida, interview by Arlene Keeling and Adam Holland, September 13, 2012. Transcript.

49 Mayo Clinic Scottsdale, "Celebrating a Decade in the Desert," 4 (Winter 1997): 1. See also Carol Attwood, "Then and Now: A Journey of Twenty Years," 10, 4 (Winter 2007): 1.

50 Ibid., 1-2.

51 Nurses from Mayo Clinic in Arizona, interview by Arlene Keeling and Adam Holland, October 2012. Transcript.

52 St. Vincent's Healthcare, "Happy 138th Birthday St. Luke's Hospital," http://www.jaxhealth.com/about-us/news/happy-birthday-st-lukes (accessed February 1, 2013).

53 Nurses from Mayo Clinic in Florida, interview by Arlene Keeling and Adam Holland, September 14, 2012. Transcript.

54 Helen Jameson, interviewed by Arlene Keeling and Adam Holland, 2012. Transcript. See also "Nurse Exchange to Benefit Hospital, Staff," *St. Luke's Hospital Today,* 5, 7 (Winter 1987). Mayo Historical Unit, Mayo Clinic in Florida, Winn Dixie Foundation Medical Library archives.

55 Mayo Medical Center Nursing Philosophy Statement, *Mayo Center for Nursing* (Spring 1991): 3.

56 Doreen Frusti, telephone interview by Arlene Keeling and Adam Holland, December 7, 2012. Transcript.

57 Department of Nursing, Mayo Clinic, "History of the Japan Nursing Exchange Program," (n.d.). Copy in the Department of Nursing, Mayo Clinic, Rochester.

58 Dianne Axen, "Progress Report—Nursing Research at Mayo Clinic," *Mayo Center for Nursing* (Winter 1993): 3.

59 Ibid., 4.

60 Nursing Research Committee Purpose Statement (n.d.). Mayo Historical Unit.

61 *Nursing Historical Highlights* (Rochester: Mayo Foundation for Medical Education and Research, 2012).

62 Doreen Frusti, telephone interview by Arlene Keeling and Adam Holland, December 7, 2012. Transcript.

63 Ibid.

64 Ibid.

65 Ibid.

66 Sharon Prinsen, "Philosophy—The Foundation of Nursing," *Mayo Center for Nursing* (Spring 1991): 4.

67 Doreen Frusti, "Nursing Directions Mayo Medical Center."

68 Ibid.

69 Beverly Parker, "Exploring the Fabric of Mayo Nursing," *Mayo Magazine* (Fall/Winter 1999): 17-24.

70 *This Week at Mayo Clinic* (July 9, 2004).

Reprint: Rochester. Mayo Historical Unit. See also Pamela Johnson, "Welcome Summer IIIs," *INSITE (Innovative Nursing Source for Information, Tips and Education)* (May 24, 2012).

71 Jasmine Ferguson (Summer III), e-mail message to Adam Holland, November 16, 2012.

Mayo Clinic nurses set the strategic goal of providing "the best nursing care in the world,"
while remaining focused on meeting the needs of each individual patient.

CHAPTER V

INTEGRATING MAYO NURSING

1992-2014

The three-shield logo represents Mayo Clinic's commitment to patient care, education, and research.

Under Doreen Frusti, R.N., nursing continued to increase in size and visibility in the organization. Nurse leaders began to populate key governance and operations committees at Mayo— an opportunity for nurse leaders to contribute to the institution's strategic direction and mission-critical priorities. The milestone would represent the realization of the long-term goal for the Department of Nursing.

If Mayo Clinic nurses were to provide "the best nursing care in the world," the organizational structure for nursing would have to focus on all shields of the institutional mission: practice, education, and research. The Department of Nursing soon modeled the Mayo Clinic committee structure, forming committees that were composed of sixty percent staff nurses, to focus on the three shields. Coming from various practice settings, they could work together on common goals, laying the foundation for professional practice.

Mayo Clinic nurses would also have to define, learn, and implement best practices to ensure quality care. Indeed, to teach and support

professional development, Mayo Clinic began to host an annual medical-surgical conference in Rochester. Other conferences would soon follow. Among these were an annual research conference held in collaboration with Winona State University and a local chapter of Sigma Theta Tau International, a nursing honor society. The conferences were key in sharing knowledge and promoting professional development for nursing.

Mayo Clinic nurses were not alone in their pursuit of quality health care. In 1992, the United States faced important policy issues related to the cost, access, and quality of medical and nursing services for its citizens.[1] In fact, when William Jefferson Clinton was elected president in November of that year, the country was in serious need of health care reform. As nursing organizations began to grapple with these issues at the national level, nursing departments at hospitals across the country also had to consider them. At Mayo Clinic, the quest to provide the best nursing care in the world would be the department's primary goal.

Also, if Mayo nurses were to give the best care in the *world*, their influence and visibility would have to reach outside the United States. As part of this effort, in 1992, Mayo nurses consulted in military hospitals across Saudi Arabia. In July 1992, Doreen Frusti and Lynn Baasch, R.N., Director of Nursing Education and Professional Development, visited Saudi Arabia, where they outlined the primary training needs for three military hospitals under the management of Witikar Saudi Arabia Limited. Later, Maria Gonyea, R.N., Assistant Nurse Manager of Pediatric Intensive Care Unit, and Anne Hotter, R.N., Clinical Nurse Specialist in Critical Care, were among other Mayo nurses who traveled to Saudi hospitals in Tabuk, Dhahran, and Hafr Al Batin to teach nurses. Once there, they learned a great deal from the Saudi nurses, particularly gaining a new respect for the customs, laws, and health practices of another culture.[2]

It was not the first time that Mayo nurses were involved in international outreach. Since the early days of the Mayo practice, Saint Marys and, later, Rochester Methodist Hospital had opened their doors to nurses from around the world, providing opportunities for the exchange of information about professional nursing practice, education, and research. Starting in the 1950s, Mayo Clinic-affiliated hospitals hosted nurses from England, Ireland, Japan, and the Philippines, along with nurses from many other countries in the Exchange Visitor's Program. The program was not an exchange of

Educational programs, such as this session in the Siebens Building at Mayo Clinic in Rochester, Minnesota, contributed to ongoing professional development of nurses.

nurses between countries; instead, it was an exchange of educational and clinical experiences in the United States.

With the high number of participants in Rochester, an organization named the "Nightingales" was founded. This group became active in the community, holding events to share different cultures through native dances, dress, and foods. The Rochester community embraced the exchange nurses by establishing the Foster Parent Program. This program offered the nurses a home away from home. It also offered friendship and served as a culture exchange while helping the nurses adjust to life in Rochester—a distinct and different culture than their own, particularly in regard to foods, weather, and finances. The program served as a link between the nurses in Rochester and their guests. It had its roots in the past, learning from other cultures and sharing knowledge had been a core Mayo value from its inception

Regional Expansion

Expanding its network within Minnesota and the neighboring states was just as important as international outreach, and in 1992, Mayo Clinic began the process of establishing a regional network of clinics, healthcare facilities, and hospitals, linking Mayo Clinic with health care providers in local communities.[3] Begun as a form of collaboration between Mayo and a six-physician practice in Decorah, Iowa, the regional network soon included larger organizations such as Midelfort

Clinic and Luther Hospital in Eau Claire, Wisconsin.[4] Ongoing expansion linked community-based providers in a relationship not only with Mayo Clinic, but also with one another.[5] By 2012, the regional network, now referred to as Mayo Clinic Health System, included more than seventy locations across the Midwest and Southeast, providing high-quality primary and specialty health care in the local communities and easy access to the resources of Mayo Clinic.[6]

With all these practices and various hospitals came not only physicians but also hundreds of nurses and allied health personnel. Incorporating them into Mayo Clinic would be the next step. Then Chair of Mayo Health System Operations (1997–2002) Peter Carryer, M.D., recalled the challenge. "Getting groups to join us was the easy and fun part… but then we realized we'd bitten off a lot and what should we do with it?" The challenge would be how best to integrate care across sites and settings, while maintaining high levels of patient safety, quality and service, and learning to operate as a single health care system rather than a dozen unique organizations.[7] Mayo's culture of collaboration would be essential to the process. So would visionary leadership on the part of nursing. In addition, the development of new technology that could connect sites via satellite and give personnel access to electronic medical records would be particularly important.

A primary care health care team collaborated at Mayo Clinic Health System in Austin, Minnesota.

For nurses throughout the system, perhaps because they were nurses and already dedicated to patients and families, there was an inherent professional bond to Mayo's focus on placing the needs of the patient first. Numerous letters sent to Mayo Clinic leaders over the next twenty years attested to the fact that Mayo Clinic Health System nurses were focused on holistic care that added a human touch. From a registered nurse in La Crosse, Wisconsin, came one story of her interactions with an elderly gentleman with lymphoma, showing how she became the comforting presence for both patient and family as he progressed through therapy. From a family of a pediatric patient in southwest Minnesota came a mother's letter, expressing her appreciation for the extra effort to alleviate her child's fears before surgery moments. Referring to the special attention the nurses had paid to their child's physiological needs, the mother noted how her daughter later said she "was so strong that she blew the OR doors open!"[8] And, from an employee of Mayo Clinic Health System in Fairmont, Minnesota, came recognition of the Emergency Department staff nurses for "making eye contact, taking extra time to get a warm blanket and giving 'detailed and caring' explanations."[9] Clearly, nurses throughout Mayo Clinic Health System were dedicated to providing patient- and family-centered care, and using individualized and age-appropriate

Angie Hammond, R.N., provided rehabilitation care for a patient at Mayo Clinic Health System-Franciscan Healthcare in La Crosse, Wisconsin.

Mayo Clinic Health System nurses benefit from the resources and activities of Mayo Clinic, but their community-based expertise would enrich the perspective of nurses and others on staff in the large referral center. Over the next twenty years, bringing nurses to Rochester for research and educational conferences and leadership team meetings, eliciting feedback and information from the regional sites, and providing other opportunities to connect to Mayo Clinic would be important to standardizing nursing practice across multiple sites, and developing the shared identity of a Mayo Clinic nurse. It would also serve to bring new ideas and methods to the greater Mayo practice.

Telemedicine and Telenursing

During the 1990s, advances in technology enhanced the ability to connect people and places. With the advent of telemedicine, connecting to remote areas of the country was becoming increasingly possible. In 1994, Mayo nurses participated in the Pine Ridge/Mayo/NASA Telemedicine Satellite Demonstration Project, providing care and education to patients at the four-bed Pine Ridge Reservation Hospital in South Dakota. Mary Trapp, R.N., was one of the leaders in the interdisciplinary twelve-week feasibility project who provided direct and indirect patient consultation as well as educational programs for allied health personnel. Mayo nurses, familiar with the teaching aspects of their role, helped with seminars on acute myocardial infarction, tuberculosis, diabetes, alcoholism, and prenatal care. The topics were all related to health problems historically common

interventions to do so.[10] Integrating them into Mayo Clinic would prove to be successful.

At the organizational level, it was somewhat more challenging to connect nurses in the Mayo Clinic Health System, many of whose practice was focused on a local community, with the larger institutional perspective of Mayo Clinic. From the start, Mayo's leaders realized that this would prove beneficial in both directions. Not only would on Indian reservations. Since the Bureau of Indian Affairs had begun to place nurses on reservations across the country in response to the 1928 Meriam Report (survey of conditions of Indian Reservations), nurses had been caring for Native American patients with trachoma, tuberculosis, heart disease, and alcoholism in remote areas where there was little access to health care.[11] Now, with the help of modern technology and the involvement of nurses with a multidisciplinary team, the resources of Mayo Clinic could be made available to people in areas far from Rochester, Minnesota.

The Closing of Saint Marys School of Practical Nursing

By the mid 1990s, hospitals throughout the country were turning to nurses who were prepared with the B.S.N. (bachelor of science in nursing), although that ideal would take years to achieve.

Saint Marys School of Practical Nursing last graduation class, 1994.

The decision was based on evidence from nursing research; with increasing patient acuity and more complex treatments and technology, it was clear that hospital nurses prepared at the baccalaureate level were better prepared to meet patient needs.[12] To implement the change in Rochester, Saint Marys School of Practical Nursing graduated its last class in 1994, the same year that Mayo Clinic announced that the organization would not be hiring any more licensed practical nurses (L.P.N.s) for inpatient bedside care.

To support staff whose jobs were affected, Mayo Clinic offered several options. The nurses could choose to accept a severance package, participate in retraining, accept a twelve-month priority placement, or enter the Enhanced Education Program to become a registered nurse (R.N.).[13] Of these, the Enhanced Education Program, which included tuition to obtain the R.N. license and the

opportunity of a staff R.N. position upon graduation, was the ideal option for many.

Mayo's emphasis would continue to be on increasing the number of registered nurses to enhance both nurse accountability and quality care.[14] The trend was occurring in hospitals throughout the country as the National Advisory Council on Nurse Education and Practice, of which Doreen Frusti was a member, recommended that health care organizations have 66 percent of their staff prepared at the bachelor's level by 2010. That goal was immediately included in Mayo Clinic's strategic plan for nursing.[15] With the new goal in mind, some Mayo Clinic licensed practical nurses accepted the offer of continuing their education with support from the Department of Nursing. Others found new and valuable roles in ambulatory care.[16]

Magnet Designation

By the late 1990s, the Department of Nursing's goals were being realized; Mayo nurses were giving excellent care and Mayo Clinic provided a supportive environment in which nurses could succeed. This achievement was recognized in 1997, when Mayo Clinic received the Magnet Award for nursing excellence from the American Nurses Credentialing Center. The award reflected the existence of a practice environment that provided opportunities for professional growth and development for nursing staff.[17] Magnet designation was important. More than two decades of research demonstrated strong evidence in the professional literature that "Magnet hospitals had significantly better work environments" than non-Magnet hospitals, and that these environments were associated with "lower levels of nurse job dissatisfaction and burnout."[18] Moreover, Magnet-recognized hospitals demonstrated "higher nurse-physician collaboration and safer work environments."[19] For Mayo Clinic nursing, Magnet status reflected values and traditions of long standing.

Certified Nurse Midwife, Emily Sisco, R.N., examined a patient at Mayo Clinic Health System in Eau Claire, Wisconsin.

Nurse-Midwives

The year 1997 was remarkable for other nursing milestones at Mayo Clinic in Rochester, as Mayo Clinic hired two certified nurse-midwives, Marie Hastings-Tolsma, R.N., and Susan Skinner, R.N. While they were the first certified nurse-midwives at Mayo Clinic in Rochester, they were not the first in Mayo Clinic Health System, where six others already were in practice. Moreover, they were not the first midwives to work with Mayo physicians in Rochester. That distinction belonged to Jane Twentyman Graham in the 1860s. Mayo's history was coming full circle. In the twenty-first century, increasing numbers of young mothers were requesting the services of nurse-midwives to provide holistic care through the birthing process.[20] Nurse-midwives could do that, supported by a team of Mayo obstetricians to whom high-risk mothers could be referred.

Mayo Clinic Hospital in Phoenix

In 1998, the first hospital planned, designed, and built by Mayo Clinic opened in Phoenix, Arizona. The 7-story, 244-bed hospital, located in the northeastern section of the city just off the interstate, would provide inpatient care for local, regional, national, and international patients. Its design supported holistic care and reflected Mayo Clinic values by providing high-tech as well as aesthetically pleasing spaces where patients and families could heal. With its spacious private rooms, beautiful artwork, state-of-the-art equipment, advanced surgical suites, and full-service emergency department, the new hospital supported Mayo Nursing's goal to provide the best nursing care in the world.

From the start, when the hospital was just scaffolding on a dirt road, nurses were involved with the planning, recommendations on

Under the leadership of Teresa Connolly, R.N., nursing practice in Arizona has evolved into a single integrated clinical department.

staff models, and the physical design of the units and equipment.[21] Working from an office building off Frank Lloyd Wright Boulevard and meeting at Mayo's campus in Scottsdale, Teresa Connolly, R.N., and Belinda Curtis, R.N., along with other Mayo nurses, worked closely with newly appointed Chief Nursing Officer Deborah Pendergast, R.N., to prepare the hospital for its grand opening.

Janete Wulsin, R.N., who had been assisting Mayo surgeons at Scottsdale Memorial North Hospital, was also part of the Mayo nursing team involved in planning the new hospital. From ordering instruments for use in urologic surgical cases to recruiting operating room nurses, she did whatever was needed to have the surgical suite ready. Collaborating with staff from other departments, she modeled "the mutual respect for every department," a key aspect of Mayo Clinic.[23] It was an exciting time, a time in which she helped form what one Mayo Clinic urologist described as "the finest urological surgical team in the world."[24]

Caring Healers in Arizona

Under the leadership of Chief Nursing Officers Deborah Pendergast, and later Teresa Connolly, nurses at Mayo Clinic in Arizona were focused on serving the best interests of the patient. Indeed, in the hospital in Phoenix, nurses sometimes mobilized other staff as well as other departments to meet specific patient and family needs. These initiatives ranged from organizing a wedding in the hospital's atrium so that the mother of the bride could attend from her intensive care unit bed to smuggling in two beloved schnauzers to meet a dying man's request to be with his pets to hosting a first wedding anniversary celebration for a seriously ill young woman who was about to start chemotherapy.[25]

Special events like these were, according to the nurses, "just what we do at Mayo Clinic."[26] In fact, they continued a long tradition of

nurses not only meeting patients' physical needs, but arranging special events to meet psychosocial needs as well. For example, in the 1950s, when Sister Amadeus Klein, R.N., was surgical supervisor at Saint Marys Hospital, she and Alfred Adson, M.D., arranged a hospital wedding for a young man who was paralyzed in a hunting accident.[27] Even prior to that time, doing whatever was needed to meet patients' needs was a hallmark of Mayo care.

Beth Gross, R.N., and Trisha Deason, R.N., provided care at the ambulatory infusion center of Mayo Clinic in Arizona.

Nursing Research

As the twentieth century drew to a close, Mayo Clinic nurses had reason to celebrate. With encouragement from Doreen Frusti and Colum Gorman, M.B., B.Ch., Ph.D., a lead researcher in endocrinology, His Royal Highness King Hussein of Jordan established the King Hussein Nursing Research Program in appreciation for the excellent nursing care he received at Mayo Clinic in Rochester. His gift made possible the goal of hiring more Ph.D. nurse researchers at Mayo Clinic. Over the next decade, several iterations of the program evolved so that nurses enrolled in Ph.D. educational programs would receive support as King Hussein Scholars.[28] This initiative provided exciting possibilities for Mayo nurses, Doreen Frusti said, "The scholarship program was important in helping the Department of Nursing achieve the Mayo three-shield model, highlighting the importance of nursing research along with practice and education."[29]

September 11, 2001

No one at Mayo Clinic—or for that matter, no one in the United States—was prepared for the horrific terrorist attacks on the World Trade Center and the U.S. Pentagon on September 11, 2001. Nearly 3,000 people were killed and 6,000 injured in the devastating attacks. The scenes were surreal and Mayo Clinic staff, like millions of people around the country, watched with horror as the events unfolded on live television newscasts. Three days later at noon on Friday, September 14, 2001, the doors of Mayo Clinic's historic Plummer Building were closed in remembrance of the victims. It was a significant and dramatic gesture. The doors of the Plummer Building were closed only on occasions of great solemnity, indicating the most profound expression of respect accorded by the institution.[30] Among the most notable occasions of their closure were the Mayo Brothers' deaths in 1939 and the assassination of President John

From left: Mayo Clinic nurses Susan Bee, R.N., Pat Anderson, R.N., Phyllis Buettner, R.N., and Louy Stambaugh, R.N., served as Red Cross mental health workers in New York City, helping survivors, families, and first responders in the aftermath of the terrorist attacks on September 11, 2001.

Kennedy in 1963.[31] Now, the closed doors symbolized Mayo Clinic's tribute to the victims and heroes of September 11, 2001.

A few weeks later, four Mayo nurses were among those who traveled to New York City to relieve mental health workers who were caring for survivors of the attacks. After weeks of nonstop work supporting families and friends of the victims, the mental health workers needed a reprieve, and once again, Mayo Clinic nurses were part of a group that would help. It was in their cultural DNA to do so.

A Nation at War

Following the attacks of September 11 the United States was once again at war, this time in Iraq and Afghanistan, and again full-time members of the Army and Navy Nurse Corps, as well as those in the Reserve, were activated to support combat missions. Numerous Mayo Clinic nurses were among those who served, and like military nurses in previous wars, they brought Mayo values and best practices into the combat arena.

Deb Jonas, R.N., served in Balad, forty miles north of Baghdad, in the 332nd Air Force Theater Hospital, a tent hospital consisting of three operating rooms, three ICUs, an ER, and five intermediate care wards with radiology, lab, and pharmacy. There, "the dust, heat and sun were incredible" and she had to protect herself the best she could while trying to "provide the best nursing care possible in those conditions."[32] According to her, "The oxygen and suction didn't just come out of the wall, you had to go and get the tank and the suction machine and make sure everything was in working order."[33] Relying on the problem-solving and communication skills she had learned at Mayo Clinic, she cared for soldiers and civilians alike. "People were the best resource over there. Everyone communicated so well with each other and it surprised me how smoothly things ran," Jonas recalled.[34]

Charles Peworski, R.N., of Mayo Clinic in Arizona, also served in Iraq, later receiving the 2004 Arizona Military Nurse of the Year

award for his heroic actions. On Easter Sunday of 2004, a blinding desert dust storm resulted in a three-vehicle high-speed crash, leaving the unit's medic injured and unable to perform his duties. Charles Peworski, relying on his nursing background and putting the needs of the patients first, ignored his own fractured arm and took control, working with another nurse to start three IVs, apply pressure dressings, stabilize fractures, treat for shock, and triage those who needed immediate care.[35] Exemplifying the role of navigator and demonstrating nursing leadership, he managed a complex situation to save lives.

Like other Mayo nurse anesthetists in previous wars, Belinda (BC) Shauver, R.N., of Mayo Clinic in Florida, relied on her triage and communication skills to make a difference. Working in Iraq in 2007, she quietly and unobtrusively pulled rank in one interaction with a rapidly deteriorating critically wounded Marine captain who insisted that his care be deferred so others in his team could be saved. As she recalls:

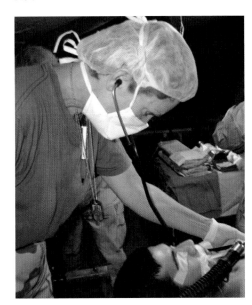

B.C. Shauver, R.N., assessed a patient's lung function while serving in Iraq.

He kept saying, "I can wait," and I finally leaned down and whispered in his ear, "Captain, this is your nurse anesthetist. I am a Navy captain, which means this is not a democracy. You need to let us take care of you." He did, in fact, quiet down, had his initial surgery, and was Med-Evac'd to Baghdad.[36]

In 2003, Mayo Clinic dedicated the *Forever Caring* sculpture in the Mayo Nurses Atrium of the Gonda Building in Rochester, honoring the nursing profession and the history of nursing at Mayo. The bronze tableau also recognized the philanthropic leadership of Warren and Marilyn Bateman, R.N., whose vision and generosity made possible the Mayo Nurses Atrium, a space beautifully decorated with marble from Spain and a Dale Chihuly glass sculpture—all part of Mayo Clinic's focus on the art, as well as the science, of healing.

The next year, the Batemans established the Bateman Clinical Instructors Fund for Nursing Education. Both knew the importance of nursing. Marilyn Bateman had been a Mayo nurse in Rochester for more than thirty years, having graduated from the Methodist-Kahler School of Nursing in 1957 and having worked in numerous positions throughout Mayo Clinic. Her husband also recognized nurses' contributions. As he noted, "Virtually every patient who comes to Mayo Clinic experiences the skill and compassion of nursing staff."[37] Now, with their generous support, Mayo Clinic leaders could now develop preeminent nursing faculty, recruit highly qualified students, and expose students to the professionalism of Mayo nursing.[38] The Batemans' gift would have a positive impact on patients, families, and nurses for generations to come.[39]

Integrating Ambulatory and Surgical Nursing

One of the most challenging aspects of the nursing integration process was the incorporation of ambulatory (outpatient) clinic nursing and surgical services into the Department of Nursing. The process would involve a fifty percent increase in the number of nursing staff in the department. It would, however, maximize utilization of nursing resources and promote a professional environment in all settings for nursing—one that would attract and retain nurses.[40] Nursing integration, an early goal of Doreen Frusti, would "support and enhance professional nursing as a clinical discipline," assuring

Forever Caring, a bronze tableau by Gloria Tew, presents the history of nursing at Mayo Clinic. It was commissioned for the Mayo Nurses Atrium in the Gonda Building on the Rochester, Minnesota, campus.

MAYO CLINIC NURSING PROFESSIONAL PRACTICE MODEL

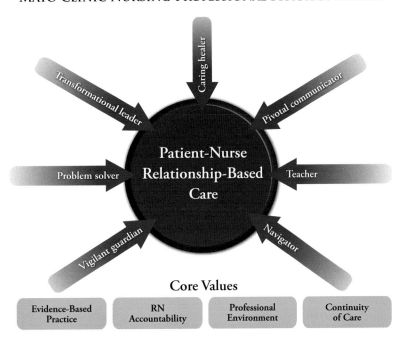

that all nursing practice at Mayo Clinic in Rochester would be "supervised and evaluated by *professional nursing.*"[41] Moreover, the integration of nursing would support specialty nursing practice across the care continuum and support a single nursing practice across Mayo sites.[42] The process would take time. It would be completed in Rochester in 2005, in Florida in 2006, and in Arizona in 2012.[43]

Mayo Nursing Care Model

In 2006, the Department of Nursing adopted the Mayo Nursing Care Model as its framework for nursing practice and roles of the nurse.[44] The model, based on Jean Watson's, Ph.D., R.N., Theory of Human Caring, along with other nurse theorists, emphasized the patient as the center of care and nurses' relationship to the patient and family, as well as to other colleagues, as radiating from that central focus. Incorporating the roles of caring healer, problem solver, navigator, teacher, pivotal communicator, vigilant guardian, and transformational leader, the model reflected all that Mayo nursing stood for, both past and present.[45] As Mayo Clinic continued to grow, integrating all of Mayo nursing would be an ongoing challenge. Each Mayo site had its own culture and nurses in each location had their own ways of doing things. To address this challenge and to define nursing care at Mayo Clinic, the Mayo Nursing Care Model which became known as the Mayo Clinic Nursing Professional Practice Model was adopted

The Mayo Clinic Nursing Professional Practice Model provided Mayo nurses at every location with shared language to define, describe and evaluate their pracice.

by all Mayo sites by 2012. The model would provide nurses throughout the Mayo system with a common language to define, describe, and evaluate their practice.[46]

Caring Healers after Hurricane Katrina

Describing Mayo nurses' work came easily as the nurses served in each of the roles outlined in the Mayo Nursing Care Model on a daily basis. On September 9, 2005, an opportunity to serve as caring healers presented itself when Mayo sent teams of health care providers, including nurses, to New Orleans to help in the aftermath of Hurricane Katrina. Only two weeks earlier, on Monday, August 29, 2005,the category-4 hurricane had slammed into the city of New Orleans. With winds of 150 miles per hour, Hurricane Katrina caused a storm surge of 25 feet, breaching the city's levees, flooding the city, and causing over $81 billion in damages along 150 miles of coastline. More than 1,800 people died, and one million people were displaced.[47]

The devastation was overwhelming. Government agencies, emergency personnel, and armed guards, as well as the National Red Cross and volunteers from throughout the world, joined the response. The health care needs of Louisiana residents were enormous; over the following days, weeks, and then months, medical and nursing volunteer teams traveled to New Orleans to help.

Nurses on team from Mayo Clinic were well prepared. Since its inception in July 1956, a committee with representatives from major departments at Mayo Clinic, Saint Marys Hospital, and Rochester Methodist had begun disaster planning. The plan involved administration, nursing, pharmacy, housekeeping, dietary, engineering, and maintenance and was focused on how medical and nursing care would be provided at the hospitals in times of disaster. In January 1976, the disaster plan became known as Code 90. The Code 90 Plan, eventually becoming the Mayo Hospital Incident Command System, was the Mayo Clinic plan for responding to both human and natural disasters, including earthquakes, floods, tornadoes, explosions, and plane crashes. Its principles could be applied anywhere in the country. Now, on September 9, 2005, the Hospital Incident Command System sent the first Mayo Clinic team, led by John Black, M.D., and Debra Hernke (Harrison), R.N., to Lafayette, Louisiana,

to assist evacuees from New Orleans. The Mayo Center was one of thirty other centers established in Region IV, under the direction of Tina Stefanski, M.D., the region's medical director.

Each day, the team on the ground and the Hospital Incident Command Center in Rochester participated in phone calls to share information and strategy. Command center leaders, representing nursing, the physician staff, administration, information technology, human resources, facilities, pharmacy, and finance would hear the report from the ground, develop strategy, identify needs, and prepare and plan for sending the next team. That plan would include supplies, staff, and logistics, and would require cooperation and collaboration from all involved.

Done in conjunction with the University of Minnesota and the College of St. Catherine, the effort was part of Operation Minnesota Lifeline, a health care relief team led by the Minneapolis-based American Refugee Committee.[48] The mission was to assess the needs of evacuees in sanctioned and unsanctioned shelters, evaluate chronic health conditions, provide immunizations, and establish primary care options for those who were unable to access health care within the overloaded system in Louisiana.[49]

Operating out of a makeshift emergency clinic set up in the Heymann Performing Arts Center in Lafayette, Mayo's first team of volunteers—including everyone from program analysts to security supervisors and photographers, from physicians and nurse practitioners to patient care assistants—worked together to meet patients' needs. Screening patients, checking blood pressures, renewing prescriptions, and immunizing more than 1,400 people for tetanus, hepatitis A,

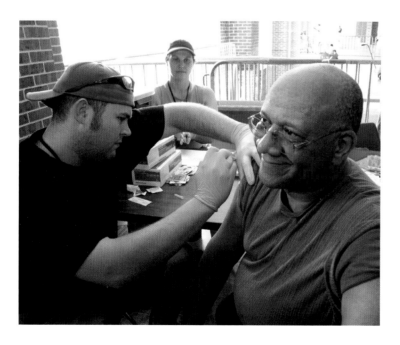

A Mayo Clinic nurse administered an immunization to a patient in Louisiana as part of Mayo's humanitarian efforts after Hurricane Katrina.

Mayo Clinic nurses and staff responded to chaotic conditions caused by Hurricane Katrina.

In 2008, Mayo Clinic was named "Best Workplace for Men in Nursing" by the American Assembly for Men in Nursing. Representing the spirit of collegiality at Mayo Clinic, Dale Pfrimmer, R.N., accepted the award with Heidi Shedenhelm, R.N.

measles, mumps, and rubella, nurses, doctors, and other personnel did what they could to help the thousands of evacuees in the area.[50] The effort would be repeated in late September and then again in October, as numerous other teams of Mayo volunteers traveled south to help.

In 2006 and 2007, Mayo teams returned to Louisiana. Working with Operation Blessing, Remote Area Medical, the International Medical Alliance, the New Orleans Health Department, and others, the Mayo teams provided free health care to thousands of needy Louisiana residents.[51] Crossing state lines and transcending barriers of race, class, and culture, Mayo staff did exactly what Dr. W. W. Mayo would have expected them to do. They responded without question to the needs of the community, putting patients' needs first.

Mayo Eugenio Litta Children's Hospital

Back in Rochester, Mayo Eugenio Litta Children's Hospital (a hospital within Saint Marys Hospital) celebrated its tenth anniversary. Since its official designation on February 19, 1996, the hospital had provided care to more than 32,940 children, some of whom had traveled from around the world to receive treatment for their complicated medical conditions. At Mayo Clinic in Rochester, nurses had long been a significant part of an interdisciplinary health care team, providing pediatric care in both the inpatient setting and in outpatient clinics, interacting with infants and children and providing support to their families. Since 2002, when Mayo was designated a Comprehensive Cancer Center, that care had increasingly included children with cancer.

Treating children with cancer was difficult for nurses, as they often saw the physical and psychosocial side effects of cancer treatment. However, in 2006, Mayo Clinic nurses learned of an opportunity to help these patients. Combining the art and science of nursing, Donna Betcher, R.N., and Julia Gourde, R.N., initiated the Beads of Courage program within the Division of Pediatric Oncology, translating into practice the findings of the nationally recognized research conducted at the University of Arizona. Adopted by more than sixty children's hospitals across the country, Beads of Courage was, as described by Jean Baruch in her dissertation on the program, "an arts-in-health program to strengthen resilience and alleviate suffering in children receiving treatment for cancer," providing the children with a symbol of accomplishment and a means to tell their story of the cancer experience.[52] In the program, a child would receive a different bead each time he or she received a transfusion, had surgery, or underwent another form of cancer treatment. White beads were for chemotherapy, glow-in-the-dark beads symbolized radiation treatment, and "courage beads" represented particularly difficult times.[53] From the nurses' point of view, seeing the smiles the beads brought to the children was one of the rewards. While not unique to Mayo Clinic, the Beads of Courage program was emblematic. Mayo nurses had long been incorporating the art of healing into their

A Mayo Clinic nurse used play therapy as part of the care program for preteen patients.

approach to individualized patient care; now in the twenty-first century, that legacy would continue.

Nursing at Mayo Clinic in Florida

In 2006, Mayo Clinic appointed Debra Harrison, R.N., as chief nursing officer for the Jacksonville campus. Building upon her long tenure at Mayo Clinic in Rochester, she was well qualified for the position, having knowledge of nursing administration and Mayo methods as well as excellent leadership and organizational skills. She received her master's degree in nursing from Winona State University and served as nurse administrator in the Department of Nursing from 2002 to 2006.[54] Of particular note, she knew how to manage disasters, having led the Mayo team in its response to Hurricane Katrina, and would be skilled in providing nursing leadership should a hurricane or other disaster occur in Jacksonville.

In 2008, Mayo Clinic opened its 214-bed hospital on the Jacksonville campus, transferring 67 patients from St. Luke's Hospital to the new facility. There, under Debra Harrison's leadership, both the patients and the newly hired nurses from the Jacksonville community would soon understand what it meant to be a Mayo Clinic nurse.

The new hospital reflected Mayo values, providing a healing environment in which state-of-the-art scientific care could be delivered without losing the focus on the patient. The hospital, with its ten-foot-wide hallways and spacious, well-equipped private rooms, modern operating rooms, full-service emergency department, electronic medical records, cutting-edge technology, and numerous specialty clinics, provided an environment conducive to professional nursing practice. The Davis Building lobby, with it rotating art exhibits, set the tone, incorporating soothing artistic touches that reflected optimism, hope, and warmth, while Louchery Island provided a peaceful outdoor space for patients, visitors, and staff to take a break.

The Florida campus provided nurses with opportunities to give the holistic patient care for which they were prepared. Guided by the principle of the patient's needs came first, nurses at Mayo Clinic in Florida, like those in Rochester and Arizona, could address psychosocial, and spiritual needs in addition to attending to physical

Debra Harrison, R.N.

needs. Often, nurses would bring humor and celebrations into their plan of care. Amanda Pendleton, R.N., an oncology nurse, recalled buying a birthday card and present for one bone marrow transplant patient to give his wife. The patient, who was being discharged to hospice care at home on his wife's birthday, wanted to make that birthday special for his wife, but he could not leave his isolation room. This gesture of caring was the "Mayo Effect" (how Mayo values come to life) in full force. When the patient asked if the nurse was allowed to do that, Amanda Pendleton replied, "Of course! This is Mayo Clinic!"[55] In another instance, she initiated a flash mob for a cancer patient, with nurses appearing seemingly out of nowhere to sing "Call Me Maybe," a song popular in 2012 by Carly Rae Jepson—just to cheer up the patient. As Amanda Pendleton, R.N., noted, knowing that "the needs of the patient come first [helps] set your priorities."[56]

Other nurses at Mayo Clinic in Florida would agree. Shirley Aina Jones, R.N., Clinical Coordinator in the Post Anesthesia Care Unit (PACU), received the Mae Berry award in 2012 for her dedication to meeting patients' needs, while Marshall Moreland, R.N., a staff nurse in the inpatient dialysis unit, was able to implement in Jacksonville the dialyzer he learned about on an educational trip to Rochester.[57] At Mayo Clinic, a staff nurse could help change practice if it was deemed in the best interest of the patient.[58]

Mayo Clinic in Florida nurses are involved in patient care, education, and research.

Patient Safety

For more than a century, nurses associated with Mayo Clinic had been concerned with patient safety—nurse anesthetists vigilantly observing respirations and heart rate in the operating room, obstetric nurses monitoring fetal distress with high-tech equipment in labor and delivery, and bedside nurses using assessments of balance, strength, and coordination as they helped a patient stand for the first time after surgery. With the release of the 1999 Institute of Medicine report, *To Err is Human: Building a Safer Health System,* Mayo nurses increased their efforts. Indeed, the report captured the attention of every health care stakeholder in the country, from health care professionals to members of the United States Congress. At the national level, the Tri-Council for nurses articulated the profession's role in addressing and preventing medical errors, emphasizing the fact

As these nurses at Mayo Clinic in Florida demonstrated, clear communication and effective handoff are vital to the continuity of patient care.

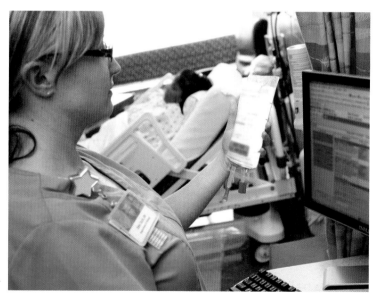

Erika Scott, R.N., ensured patient safety by verifying that the appropriate medication was given to the right patient.

that multidisciplinary teams, including nurses, would have to work together to provide patients with the best care possible.[59] By 2010, long dedicated to providing the best nursing care in the world, Mayo nurses were involved with numerous new patient safety initiatives, including patient fall assessment and prevention, enhanced monitoring for surgical patients, arm band standardization, bar code medication and documentation, and bedside rounds/safety checklists. Chief among these were nurse-to-nurse bedside handoffs using a standardized communication framework that involved an introduction of the oncoming nurse, discussion of the patient's progress, plan of care for the next shift, and the opportunity for the patient or family to ask questions.[60]

Mayo One, 2011

Part of connecting patients and health care providers in Mayo Clinic Health System and breaking down geographical barriers to care depended on the medical transport teams that could respond to emergencies throughout the system. Since 1984, Mayo Clinic in Rochester had used Mayo One, an emergency medical helicopter that could respond to calls within a 150-mile radius of the city. Later, in 1994, Mayo added a fixed-wing aircraft (based in Rochester) so that patient transports could be made worldwide. By 2002, the helicopter service also included helicopters based in Mankato, Minnesota, and Eau Claire, Wisconsin.

The nurses who worked as part of the Mayo One emergency response teams provided healing interventions in dramatic life-saving moments. According to Dan Mueller, R.N., Mayo One staff nurse since the program started in 1984, the Mayo One team (consisting of emergency nurses who were also part of the code team) relied on "the most basic of life support measures, including intravenous fluids, EKG monitoring through the tiny oscilloscope of Lifepack 5, oxygen and drugs such as atropine, epinephrine, lidocaine and dilantin."[61]

Over the years, the Mayo One response program and the helicopter's equipment evolved dramatically. In 2011, when Mayo One transported Cole, a young boy crushed in a tractor accident on

Mayo nurses and paramedics are always ready to fly within moments notice on the emergency medical helicopter. From left: Kathy Berns, R.N., Tricia Holden, Paramedic, Raquel (Kelly) Sahs, R.N., Bridget Berry R.N., and Mary Svoboda, R.N.

his family's farm, the helicopter was equipped with advanced respiratory medical equipment such as bi-level positive airway pressure (BIPAP) and mechanical ventilators, high-tech laboratory capabilities, and multiple medications to treat almost any medical condition. The team had the advanced clinical skills to intubate, insert chest tubes, perform emergency surgical airways, and give plasma and blood products.[62]

Kimberly Arndorfer, R.N., and Jeffrey Sterns, R.N., were part of Cole's response team. Both had years of experience in critical care and were expert clinicians. Recalling the evening of Cole's rescue, Kimberly Arndorfer noted that their "collective critical care experience" was a factor in Cole's survival. Having been crushed by the tractor and bleeding internally from the liver, in addition to suffering from a collapsed lung, Cole was in critical condition when the Mayo One team arrived in the muddy field. Quickly assessing his condition and their surroundings, the team decided to transport Cole to the hospital in Eau Claire, a ten-minute air transport, rather than inserting a chest tube in the field or while flying to Rochester. Kimberly Arndorfer explained her decision:

Just because you know you can do something, like insert a chest tube, doesn't mean it's the best idea at the time. Cole was lying in a muddy,

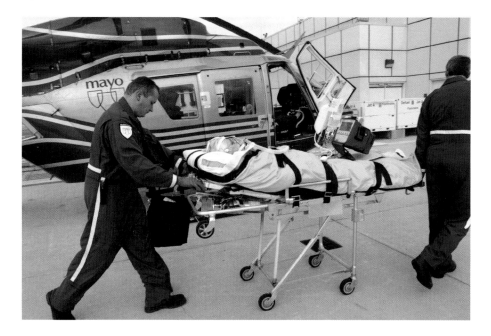

For nurses on the Mayo One *emergency response team, collaboration, vigilant observation, and clinical acumen are vital. As one nurse explained, "You have to rely on the pilot to get you there and back, and your colleagues to help you evaluate the patient and begin the treatment."*

thinking. As Dan Mueller, R.N., and Kathy Berns, R.N., both noted, "You can't hear lung sounds over the roar of the helicopter, so you have to rely on other clinical indicators such as the patient's color, the oxygen saturation levels and the rise and fall of the chest.[64] Their care was reminiscent of that of Saint Marys' nurse anesthetists a century earlier. They, too, had to rely on vigilant observation and clinical acumen to assess the patient and determine what interventions might be necessary.

Teamwork and collaboration were also hallmarks of Mayo One rescue efforts. As clinical nurse specialist Kathy Berns, R.N., noted, both are important in situations such as rappelling down the cliffs of a river bed to rescue a canoeist in critical condition. "You have to rely on the fireman supporting your ropes, the pilot to get you there and back, and your colleagues to help you evaluate the patient and begin the treatment."[65]

manure-covered field; it was dusk and getting colder. We knew he needed a chest tube. We also knew it would be better for him to have it inserted under better circumstances—in the Emergency Department at Eau Claire, 10 minutes away by air—under sterile conditions, by a pediatric trauma surgeon using a pediatric-sized tube. Cole was still conscious and talking somewhat. Relying on our years of experience in critical care, we used our best judgment and left for Eau Claire. Once he was stabilized, we could head to Rochester.[63]

Skilled in clinical assessment and in the prioritization of patient needs, as well as personalizing Cole's care to the situation, the flight nurses acted decisively. It was a brave decision based on years of clinical experience.

Flying at altitudes commonly around 2,500 feet, flight nurses had to rely both on their clinical assessment skills and their critical

Visionary Leadership

In 2011, Doreen Frusti, retired as chair of the Department of Nursing and Mayo Clinic chief nursing officer. Pamela Johnson, R.N., was named Chair, Department of Nursing in Rochester and Mayo Clinic Chief Nursing Officer. She was well positioned to lead and build a unified nursing practice across all Mayo sites. Her education included a bachelor's degree in nursing from the College of St. Catherine and a master's degree in nursing from the University of Minnesota. She also was experienced with Mayo and its methods, having worked in various roles at Mayo Clinic since 1980; beginning in 2005, she had served as vice chair of the Department of Nursing, responsible for all clinical nursing across both the inpatient and ambulatory practices. In that role and in collaboration with Doreen Frusti, R.N., she led the establishment of a council/committee structure to standardize nursing care processes, policies, and procedures throughout the Mayo system. Chief among these had been the standardization of management of pressure ulcers and falls prevention, and the diffusion of nurse-to-nurse bedside handoffs.

In one of her first all-staff meetings, Pamela Johnson set the future direction for Mayo nursing, describing the time as one with unprecedented opportunity to influence the direction of health care on behalf of patients and families by redefining the role of nursing through "care redesign."[66] Her assessment of the new opportunities for nursing at Mayo Clinic aligned with the profession's views at the national level. Just the year before, in 2010, the Institute of Medicine had published a report on nursing based on a two-year initiative with the Robert Wood Johnson

From left: Pamela Johnson, R.N., chair, and Amy Zwygart, R.N., vice chair, lead strategic initiatives for the Department of Nursing across all Mayo Clinic locations. As Pamela Johnson explained, "The Mayo Effect begins with each of us, individually and collectively, keeping the needs of our patients first."

LEADERSHIP

"Never underestimate the impact that one individual can have on another. Every interaction makes an impression. Our patients and families look to each of you to provide hope and healing, to inspire trust, and to provide that unparalleled care experience that Mayo Clinic promises."

PAMELA JOHNSON, R.N.

Foundation. The report, *The Future of Nursing: Leading Change, Advancing Health,* pointed to barriers preventing nurses from "being able to respond effectively to rapidly changing health care settings" and called for nurses to practice to the "full extent of their education and training."[67] The report also called for nurses to be full partners in clinical teams. Once again, a national report reaffirmed Mayo traditions and Mayo values. Nurses had long been considered valuable members of the Mayo health care team. Now, Pamela Johnson, reminded her staff of their heritage, noting, "The Mayo Effect begins with each of us, individually and collectively, keeping the needs of our patients first."[68]

Building on a long history in which Mayo Clinic nurses made a difference one patient at a time, she would take Mayo nursing to a new level. Her goal was to ensure physician-administrator-nursing partnerships at all levels, defining "nursing care models for the future that would leverage nursing contributions to Mayo's strategic priorities."[69] In 2011, Amy Zwygart, R.N., was named Vice Chair, Department of Nursing in Rochester. She would be accountable for all clinical nursing practice at Mayo Clinic in Rochester, providing leadership to assure a consistent model of nursing care and transforming the Mayo mission and principles into daily operation. This leadership team would ensure the realization of the Mayo Effect within the Department of Nursing.

Top, from left: Ritu Banerjee, M.D., certified physician assistant Lester Kiemele and Robin Georgeff, R.N., were among the Mayo Clinic colleagues who provided care to survivors of a devastating earthquake in Haiti in 2011.
Bottom right: Robin Georgeff, who practices at Mayo Clinic in Arizona, bonded with youngsters in Port-au-Prince.

Responding to an Earthquake

The Mayo Effect would soon spread to other parts of the world as Mayo nurses responded to the effects of a devastating earthquake. In February 2011, Mayo nurses went to Haiti where they collaborated with Operation Blessing International and St. Damien's Children's Hospital to help set up a functional emergency room and establish a clinic. Working with Father Rick Frechette, a Catholic priest and physician who was struggling to meet the desperate need for health care services, Mayo Clinic volunteers, including three nurse practitioners, three physicians, and three to four other nurses did what they could to help.[70]

Team members focused on building a sustainable program. They not only provided direct care but also educated local providers about how to continue the work when Mayo and other volunteers returned home. Their initiative included more than caring for trauma patients. Cholera was a major problem and the clinic staff often saw twenty to thirty cholera patients a day. Finding best solutions to the problem of rehydrating cholera patients in the poverty-stricken community was challenging. A team member recalled that nurses used what they had on hand; fluids were given by mouth rather than intravenously, and tin buckets served as commodes. Like other Mayo nurses in wartime and in epidemics, these colleagues used innovative solutions to address problems.

Nurse Anesthetists

By 2012, Mayo Clinic's Nurse Anesthesia Program, had the distinction of being the oldest continuously operating school of nurse anesthesia in the United States. Now, however, in contrast to the original

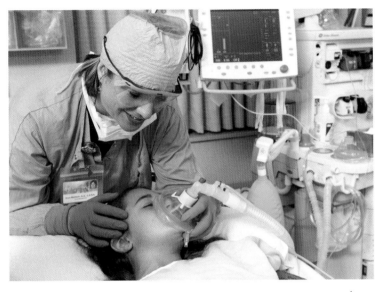

Certified Nurse Anesthetist, Jean Mattson, R.N., administered anesthesia to a patient.

members would work to"the full extent of their licensure," she would provide Mayo Clinic nurses with the support they needed to "provide the right care, at the right time, in the right location, with the right provider."[71] This would be the culmination of 150 years of nursing service and position nursing at Mayo Clinic for national and global leadership amid the challenges of the twenty-first century.

apprenticeship model under Drs. Will and Charlie, the thirty-month degree program, awarding a master's of nurse anesthesia, was accredited by the Council on Accreditation of Nurse Anesthesia Education Programs. Requiring a bachelor's degree in nursing with at least one year of clinical intensive care unit experience for admission, the program consisted of extensive course work in collaboration with Winona State University, clinical internships in all subspecialty areas of anesthesia, and an eight-week rotation to various Mayo Clinic sites.

Mayo Nursing: A Single Practice and Common Identity
Pamela Johnson articulated a vision to lead Mayo nursing into the future. As she noted in 2012, one of her priorities would be to focus "on deliberate action items to move toward a single, standardized nursing practice" across all sites and the continuum of care, "with the goal of improving the safety, services and outcomes" for all Mayo Clinic patients. "Leveraging resources" so that all team

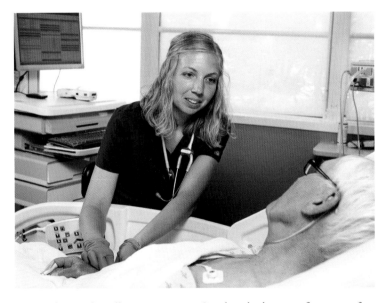

The tradition of excellence continues. One hundred twenty-five years after Edith Graham, R.N., taught the Franciscan Sisters the basics of nursing when St. Mary's Hospital opened in 1889, nurses remain key contributors to practice, education, and research at Mayo Clinic.

ENDNOTES

1 Pamela Maraldo and Claire Fagin, "The Nurses' National Health Plan," in *Charting Nursing's Future: Agenda for the 1990s,* Linda Aiken and Claire Fagin, 505 (New York: J. B. Lippincott Company, 1992).

2 Kristin Clouse, "Mayo Nurses Teach in Saudi Arabia," *Mayo Today* (June/July 1993).

3 Michelle Hedin and Amy Zwygart, "Getting to Know the Mayo Health System" (PowerPoint presentation, March 2012).

4 Peter Carryer and Sylvester Sterioff, "Mayo Health System: A Decade of Achievement," *Mayo Clinic Proceedings,* 78, 8 (August 2003): 1047-1053.

5 Megan Marugani, *Heritage Project.* Mayo Clinic.

6 "Mayo Clinic Health System: 20 Years of Benefiting Area Communities," *This Week at Mayo Clinic* (April 27, 2012).

7 Marugani, *Heritage Project.*

8 See Mayo Clinic Health System nurse exemplars (2012). Specific identification withheld for patient confidentiality.

9 Ibid.

10 Ibid.

11 Thomas Kottke, Leonard Little Finer, Mary Trapp, Laurel Panser, and Paul Novotny, "The Pine Ridge-Mayo National Aeronautics and Space Administration Telemedicine Project: Program Activities and Participant Reactions," *Mayo Clinic Proceedings,* 71, 4 (April 1996): 329-337. For further reading on the topic of Indian health care, see Arlene Keeling, Chapter 4: "My Treatment was Castor Oil and Aspirin: Field Nursing among the Navajo People in the Four Corners Region, 1925-1955," *Nursing and the Privilege of Prescription, 1893-2000* (Columbia: The Ohio State University Press,

2007): 72-96. Since the publication of the Meriam Report in 1928, the United States government had begun to place field matrons on the reservations with public health nurses. Among the American Indians, the incidence of tuberculosis and trachoma was high.

12 Linda Aiken, S. Clarke, R. Cheung, D. Sloane, and J. Silber, "Educational Levels of Hospital Nurses and Surgical Patient Mortality," *Journal of the American Medical Association,* 290, 12 (2003):1617-1623.

13 Ibid.

14 *Nursing Historical Highlights* (Rochester: Mayo Foundation for Medical Education and Research, 2012): 13.

15 Adam Holland, e-mail communication with Arlene Keeling, January 2013.

16 Mark Denis P. Davis, *Mayo Clinic Dermatology: The First Ninety Years* (Rochester: Mayo Foundation for Medical Education and Research, 2007): 142.

17 Nicole Sisk, "Magnet Profession, People," *Mayo Today* (December 2002-January 2003): 8-9, quote p. 8.

18 Lesley Kelly, Matthew McHugh, and Linda Aiken, "Nurse Outcomes in Magnet and Non-Magnet Hospitals," *Journal of Nursing Administration,* 41, 10 (October 2011): 428-433.

19 K. Armstrong, H. Laschinger, C. Wong, "Workplace Empowerment and Magnet Hospital Characteristics as Predictors of Patient Safety Climate," *Journal of Nursing Administration,* 39 (2009): S17-S24.

20 "Increased Interest Causes Mayo to Add Two Nurse Midwives," *Post-Bulletin* (June 30, 1997).

21 Teresa Connolly, interview by Arlene Keeling and Adam Holland, October 26, 2012. Transcript .

22 Ibid.

23 Janete Wulsin, R.N., (Mayo Clinic in Arizona), interview by Arlene Keeling and Adam Holland, October 26, 2012. Transcript.

24 Nurses from Mayo Clinic in Arizona, interview by Arlene Keeling and Adam Holland, October 26, 2012. Transcript.

25 Ibid.

26 Ibid.

27 Sister Amadeus Klein, Kate Towey, and Virginia Wentzel, "Nursing History—Neurological and Neurosurgical Hospital Nursing," *Mayo Foundation:*15.

28 King Hussein Scholars Program, brochure, Mayo Clinic.

29 Doreen Frusti, interview by Arlene Keeling and Adam Holland, December 7, 2012.Transcript.

30 "Plummer Doors" (posted January 10, 2012). Mayo Clinic.

31 Ibid. The doors would be closed again in January 2012 in a ceremony broadcast at the Florida Mayo Clinic site in remembrance of Dr. Luis Bonitta, M.D., organ procurement technician, David Hines, and the pilot of a helicopter that crashed during a trip to procure a heart for transplant.

32 Deb Jones, R.N., as quoted in a story submitted by Sandra Miller, R.N., Mayo Clinic.

33 Ibid.

34 Ibid.

35 Margarita Gore, "A Follow-up Story," *Vital Link,* 8 (March 2005): 1. See also "Winner: Arizona Military Nurse of the Year, 2004." Reprint: Rochester. Mayo Clinic.

36 Belinda Curtis, e-mail message to Adam Holland, January 23, 2013.

37 Warren and Marilyn Bateman, "Honoring the Nurses at Mayo Clinic." Mayo Clinic story.

38 Ibid.

39 Ibid.

40 "Nursing Integration Update OPC/HPC Joint Meeting" (March 24, 2003). Mayo Clinic.

41 Ibid.

42 Ibid. See also Michael Muehlenbein, "Nursing Integration at Mayo" (PowerPoint Presentation, December 11, 2002).

43 Various dates are given for the integration in Florida, but it is clear that the major effort occurred under Deb Harrison's leadership in 2006. It was further implemented in 2008 when the new hospital opened on the Florida campus. See Deb Harrison, e-mail message to Adam Holland, January 23, 2013.

44 Adam Holland, e-mail message to Arlene Keeling, January 23, 2013.

45 See Mayo Clinic, "Mayo Nursing Care Model: Principles and Roles" (2008).

46 Adam Holland, email message to Arlene Keeling, January 23, 2012. See also "Mayo Clinic Nursing Care Model," excerpt from Mayo Clinic Nursing Executive Committee Meeting (June 28 and 29, 2012).

47 Theresa O'Neill and Patricia Prechter, Chapter 12: "A Tale of Two Shelters: A Katrina Story, 2005," in Barbra Wall and Arlene Keeling, eds. Nurses on the Front Line: When Disaster Strikes, 1878-2010 (New York: Springer Publishing Company, 2011).

48 Mary Pattock, "Hurricane Katrina: When the World Changed...and SON Faculty Made a Difference," Minnesota Nursing (Spring 2006): 20-21.

49 Debra Harrison (Chief Nursing Officer, Mayo Clinic in Florida), interview by Arlene Keeling and Adam Holland, September 2012. Transcript. See also Debra Harrison, R.N., "Project: Minnesota Lifeline" (draft, Sept 23, 2005).

50 Mayo Clinic Responds—Hurricane Katrina Relief. DVD (Rochester, MN: Mayo Clinic, 2005). See also Debra Harrison (Chief Nursing Officer, Mayo Clinic in Florida), interview by Arlene Keeling and Adam Holland, September 2012. Transcript.

51 Staci Dennis, "Volunteers Help Make Medical Event a Success," Operation Blessing International, www.ob.org/programs/disaster_relief/news/2007/dr_2007_0416_NOWeiss.asp (accessed September 4, 2012). See also John Patrick, "OBI Wraps Up Katrina Efforts, Helps 2.7 Million People," Operation Blessing International, www.ob.org/programs/disaster/news/2008/dr_2008_0215_katrina_finale.asp (accessed September 4, 2012).

52 Jean Baruch, "The Beads of Courage Program for Children Coping with Cancer," (Dissertation [from abstract], University of Arizona).

53 "Beads of Courage," In the Loop (August 18, 2011).

54 Debra Harrison (formerly Hernke), curriculum vitae, Mayo Clinic.

55 Amanda Pendleton, R.N. (Mayo Clinic in Florida), interview by Arlene Keeling and Adam Holland, September, 2012. Transcript.

56 Ibid.

57 Adam Holland, "Meeting Notes" (meeting with Arlene Keeling and nurses, Mayo Clinic in Florida, September 14, 2012): 1-2.

59 Nurses from Mayo Clinic in Florida, interviewed by Arlene Keeling and Adam Holland, September 14, 2012. Transcript.

58 Tri-Council for Nursing, "Response to the Institute of Medicine's Report—'To Err is Human: Building a Safer Health System," in Arlene Keeling, Barbara Brodie, and John Kirchgessner, The Voice of Professional Nursing Education: A 40-Year History of the American Association of Colleges of Nursing, 93 (Washington, D.C.: AACN, 2010).

59 Mayo Clinic, Department of Nursing, 2009 Division Highlights, Orthopedics/Radiology Division (2009).

60 Ibid.

61 Ibid.

64 Ibid.

65 Pamela Johnson, "Comments on Chapter 5" (November, 2012).

66 Institute of Medicine, The Future of Nursing: Leading Change, Advancing Health (IOM and Robert Wood Johnson Foundation, 2010).

67 Pamela Johnson, "Remarks to All Staff Meeting" (January 2011). Reprint: Rochester.

68 Adam Holland, e-mail message to Arlene Keeling, January 2013.

69 Gordon Griffin, YouTube website.

70 Mayo Clinic (PowerPoint presentation, October 21, 2011); see also Pamela Johnson, "More on Mayo Clinic in the Midwest," Leadership (April 26, 2012).

71 Ibid.

"I look through a half-opened door
into the future, full of interest, intriguing
beyond my power to descibe, but
with a full understanding that it is
for each generation to solve its own problems
and that no man has the wisdom
to guide or control the next generation."

William J. Mayo

— William James Mayo, M.D.
1931

AN INSPIRING JOURNEY:
MAYO CLINIC NURSING LOOKS TO THE FUTURE

By Pamela O. Johnson, R.N.
Mayo Clinic Chief Nursing Officer

The story of Mayo Clinic for the past 150 years is an inspiring journey of what is possible when physicians, nurses, and other care team members work together with the shared commitment that the needs of the patient come first. This value will guide us into an equally inspiring future.

While there are many factors that have and will continue to contribute to our Mayo nursing heritage, a few key success factors are especially noteworthy. The first is having a vision of what nursing's unique role is and can be in a constantly changing health care environment. This vision is expressed in the roles that are described in the Mayo Clinic Nursing Care Model: caring healer, problem solver, navigator, teacher, pivotal communicator, vigilant guardian, and transformational leader—all of which have been highlighted throughout this book.

Second, for nurses to succeed in providing care that leverages their talents, skills, and knowledge, a professional environment must be present. Mayo Clinic recognizes and supports nursing as a distinct professional discipline. Led by a Mayo Clinic chief nursing officer, nurses have the authority and accountability for their discipline. To that end, our steady journey to a single integrated nursing practice has been critically important. This journey started with the integration of the ambulatory, inpatient, and surgical nursing practice in Rochester, moved to Mayo Clinic sites in Arizona and Florida, and now includes the Mayo Clinic Health System. Our efforts have resulted in the full integration of Mayo Clinic nursing with a common care model and standard of nursing practice that follows the patient throughout the continuum of care.

A third hallmark of Mayo Clinic nursing is the designation of nursing as a clinical department consistent with other Mayo Clinic medical and surgical physician departments. Like these departments, nursing is a "three-shield discipline," with robust activities in patient care, education, and research, all of which are depicted in the three shields of the Mayo Clinic logo. Our commitment to excellence in *practice* is at the core of what Mayo nurses do, providing evidence-based care to patients. Our *education* is multifaceted with an orientation program that creates a sound knowledge base, clear expectations, and successful transition into the Mayo Clinic practice environment; a competency program that assures nurses have the skills to care for patients today and into the future; and professional development opportunities supporting lifelong learning and professional development. Our nursing *research* fosters an environment of scientific inquiry as nurse scientists generate new knowledge and help staff better identify and incorporate evidence-based practice as the foundation of all nursing care to improve patient care and outcomes.

As Mayo Clinic partners with other health care organizations to develop the Mayo Clinic Care Network, nursing has an opportunity to share key success factors and generate new knowledge with our nursing colleagues across the globe. Nurses will continue to be a vital and important part of the growth and evolution of Mayo Clinic.

What does the future of Mayo Clinic nursing hold? While caring for the sick will always be a sacred part of what we do, health care has now advanced to the point where consumers look to nurses to help them get and stay healthy and independently manage their health and chronic conditions. All along the life cycle, from prenatal care to end-of-life care, Mayo Clinic nurses meet the wide-ranging physical, spiritual, and emotional needs of patients and families while providing knowledge, hope, and human touch. Going forward, we must also incorporate the quickly progressing world of informatics and technology into our care, while using data to provide information at the point of care to assist nursing assessment, judgment, and decision making. We will continue to explore technology and the opportunities it presents to connect with patients and consumers to meet their individual needs, in many cases bringing care to them, wherever they are. Most importantly, we will continue to measure outcomes to demonstrate the added value that nurses bring to the patients we care for, the health care experience, and shape the future of health care.

I would like to thank the nursing staff, past and present, for always putting the needs of the patient first, the stories they shared, and most importantly, the inspiration they demonstrate; to the Nursing History Committee for their idea to document our history; to Arlene Keeling, Ph.D., R.N., F.A.A.N., who did a masterful job of capturing "our" story through hours of research, interviews, and writing. I would also like to acknowledge Adam Holland, R.N., whose constant attention, coordination, and project management made this book possible; to Matthew Dacy for his wisdom and expert guidance throughout this process; to Karen Barrie for her beautiful design; to Amy Zwygart, R.N., and Kristine Johnson, R.N., for their insight and advice; to the many friends and supporters of this project; and to those listed on page 139 who were part of the team helping to ensure historical accuracy. To each of you, I express my profound deep gratitude. A special thank you to our benefactors: John P. Guider, Saint Marys Hospital Auxiliary Volunteers; John T. Blozis through the Anna Blozis Fund for Nursing at Saint Marys Hospital; Rochester Methodist Hospital Auxiliary Volunteers; and Methodist-Kahler School of Nursing Alumni Association, whose generosity helped make the long-held dream and publication of this book a reality.

Mayo Clinic draws nurses who want to work in a professional, interdisciplinary, and scientifically stimulating environment where their knowledge, skills, commitment, pride, and passion are demonstrated and recognized every day, touching patients and families in ways that they may not even realize. None of this would be possible without an organizational culture that recognizes and supports nursing as a key professional partner, especially in our complex multisite academic practice. I am deeply grateful to our leaders and colleagues throughout Mayo Clinic for their support, encouragement, and recognition of nursing as an integral part of the health care team.

The beautiful facilities, advanced technology, and dedicated colleagues are all important. However, it is our patients and families, with their hopes and needs, goals and dreams, who inspire nurses to deliver the best care every day. Ultimately, this book is made possible by—and dedicated to—the patients of Mayo Clinic.

While we know that health care has many challenges ahead, the role and future of professional nursing has never been more exciting. I am confident that the future stories describing the contributions of nursing and its influence on the care of our patients will be every bit as exciting as the first 150 years.

What a honor and a privilege it is to be a nurse at Mayo Clinic.

Pamela O. Johnson

AUTHOR'S REFLECTIONS

Having responded to a call for proposals to write the 150-year history of nursing at Mayo Clinic, I was honored when I received an email in early January, 2012 informing me that I had been chosen to do so! Excited by the opportunity, I began to read every history I could find about Mayo Clinic and its famous physicians, aware that it would be a daunting task to learn about 150 years of the Clinic, discover the nurses' stories, and then write a narrative that would be interesting to the general public as well as to the medical and nursing community. The need to complete the manuscript in just one calendar year made the task even more challenging, so I was delighted to discover that I would be working with a team of Mayo historians, archivists, nurses, administrators, and graphic designers. In fact, our first team meeting demonstrated to me that Mayo Clinic leaders lived their values. They did not just talk about "team work," they did it! The fact that they were also extremely professional made the entire process a pleasure.

From my first read of the secondary sources about the Doctors Mayo, I was fascinated. After immersing in the primary data from the Mayo Historical Unit, the archives in Saint Marys Hospital and the Methodist-Kahler Alumni room, I began to see nursing's role in the story. By the time I was writing that Sister Mary Joseph, Dr. Will, and Dr. Charlie Mayo died in 1939, I was in tears. Mayo Clinic's nursing history had come to life for me, and I wanted to share it.

From then on, the narrative flowed. Starting with the idea that Louise Abigail Mayo no doubt served as Dr. William Worrall Mayo's first "nurse," I documented countless stories about how the Sisters of Saint Francis, later the nursing students from the Mayo-affiliated schools of nursing, and finally contemporary nurses were involved on the Mayo team. The challenge was trying to be selective of stories and photographs that would resonate with alumni, visitors, patients, current nurses, and other health care providers, while at the same time capturing the major events of the past 150 years. Hopefully I have done that, and you will be able to find a section of the book that reflects your memories of your time at Mayo Clinic, your particular campus (including those in Arizona, Florida, and Mayo Clinic Health System), your experiences in various specialties and clinical units, or your involvement in Mayo's local, regional, national, and global community.

Thank you to the entire team for their confidence in me and for their support during the process and to all who participated in interviews. A special thanks to Adam Holland, R.N., without whose help, research assistance, and guidance, this book would not have come to fruition.

Arlene W. Keeling

—Arlene W. Keeling, R.N., Ph.D., F.A.A.N

Acknowledgments

With appreciation to these colleagues, whose support and expertise

played a key role in the publication of this book.

Vaunette Alrick, R.N.

Michelle Alore, R.N.

Trish Amundson

Kimberly Arndorfer, R.N.

Noel Arring, R.N.

Kenna Atherton

Carol Ann Attwood

Nicole Babcock

Dorothy Bell, R.N.

Christina Berger, R.N.

Debra Berland, R.N.

Kathleen Berns, R.N

Marguerite Brenner, R.N.

Tara Brigham

Karen Brommer

Jane Campion, R.N.

Jessica Charles, R.N.

Barbara Cleary, R.N.

Teresa Connolly, R.N.

Doralyn Costello, R.N.

Belinda Curtis, R.N.

Cynthia Danner, R.N.

Patrick Dean, R.N.

Kathryn Deisher

Jasmine Ferguson

Mark Fratzke, R.N.

Doreen Frusti, R.N.

W. Bruce Fye, M.D.

Sister Generose Gervais

Monte Gulliford, R.N.

Debra Harrison, R.N.

Angela Herron

Jean Higgins, R.N.

Christine Hindt

Diane Holmay, R.N.

Anne Hudgens, R.N.

Ann Ihrke

Janice Jacobson, R.N.

Helen Jameson, R.N.

Janis Johnson, R.N.

LeAnn Johnson, R.N.

Shirley Aina Jones, R.N.

Donna Kalkines, R.N.

Jean Keane

Carmen Keller

Barbara Kermisch

Mark LaMaster, R.N.

Susan Launder, R.N.

Troy Lindloff

Jennifer Lofgren, R.N.

Connie Luedtke, R.N.

Julie Lundberg, R.N.

Linda Marchildon, R.N.

Patti Marshock, R.N.

Suzanne Mattson, R.N.

Kimberly Mazur, R.N.

Peter McConahey

Teresa Mercer, R.N.

Anne Miers, R.N.

Sandra Moore, R.N.

Marshall Moreland, R.N.

Daniel Mueller, R.N.

Sister Antoine Murphy, R.N.

Charlyn Myatt, R.N.

Barbara Myhre

Billie Needham

Laura Nero, R.N.

Carolyn O'Brien, R.N.

Nancy Panthofer, R.N.

Amanda Pendleton, R.N.

Sister Mary Lonan Reilly

Tyson Robinson

Jennifer Roslien, R.N.

Jennifer Sabyan, R.N.

Erika Scott, R.N.

Suzanne Shaw, R.N.

Linda Sorensen, R.N.

Jennifer Steinberg, R.N.

Susan Stirn, R.N.

Sharon Tennis, R.N.

Sandra Toogood

Margaret Turk R.N.

Diane Twedell, R.N.

Sandra Ventro

Mary Volcheck, R.N.

Carol Ann Wallace, R.N.

Sister Lau ns Wentzel, R.N.

Sister Ellen Whelan, Ph.D.

Pamela White, R.N.

Naomi Whiteman, R.N.

Kelly Wise, R.N.

Diane Salentiny Wrobleski, R.N.

Janete Wulsin, R.N.

Kathleen Zarling, R.N.

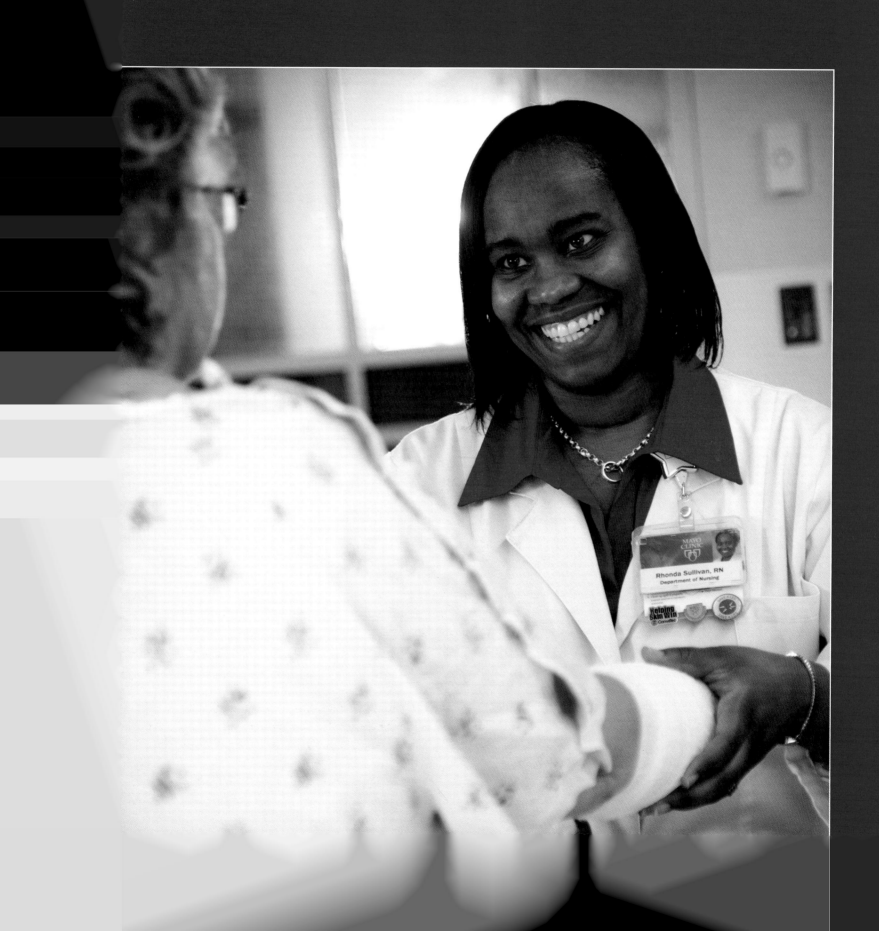

A Timeline of Mayo Clinic Nursing

By Adam Holland, R.N.

Mayo Clinic Nursing Administrative Specialist

1851—Louise Abigail Wright married William Worrall Mayo (Dr. W.W. Mayo) and began assisting her husband's medical practice when needed. Their youngest son, Charles H. Mayo, M.D. (Dr. Charlie), later recalled, "Mother was a real good doctor herself." Given the nature of her work, it is also appropriate to say that Louise Mayo demonstrated many qualities of excellence in nursing.

1863—Dr. W.W. Mayo was appointed by President Abraham Lincoln as examining surgeon for the Union Army, based in Rochester, Minnesota.

1864—Dr. W.W. Mayo settled his family in Rochester and announced he was opening a private medical practice. Mayo Clinic dates its origin to the start of this practice.

1883—William J. Mayo (Dr. Will) obtained his M.D. degree from the University of Michigan and joined his father in practice.

Thirty-seven people died, more than 200 were injured, and one-third of Rochester was destroyed when one of the largest and strongest tornadoes in Minnesota history left a 25-mile destructive path through the city and the surrounding country side. Needing help to care for the wounded survivors, Dr. W.W. Mayo worked with Mother Alfred Moes and the Franciscan Sisters, a local Catholic teaching order. After the crisis passed, Mother Alfred came to Dr. W.W. Mayo with a bold plan: The Franciscan Sisters would fund the construction of a hospital and serve as nurses if the Doctors Mayo would provide medical care. Hesitant at first, Dr. Mayo accepted her proposal, establishing a collaborative relationship that continues to shape Mayo Clinic today.

1888—Charles H. Mayo (Dr. Charlie) obtained his M.D. degree from Northwestern University and joined his father and brother in practice.

1889—Dr. W.W. Mayo hired Edith Graham, R.N., a recent graduate of the nursing program at Women's Hospital in Chicago, to assist with the medical practice, becoming the first professionally trained nurse in Rochester.

After many years of hard work, frugal living, and careful saving, the Sisters of Saint Francis opened St. Mary's Hospital. The 3 story building, with 3 wards and 1 private room, had 27 beds.

Edith Graham, R.N., taught basic skills of nursing care to the Sisters of Saint Francis, who were trained as teachers. Some of the skills she taught included assessing patients, taking vital signs, changing surgical dressings, and administering medications.

Mother Alfred Moes called Sister Joseph Dempsey from her teaching position in Kentucky to become a nurse at St. Mary's Hospital. In her subsequent 47-year career, Sister Joseph served as the hospital superintendent and first surgical assistant to Dr. Will, playing a key role in the discovery of a metastatic nodule of the umbilicus, later known as "Sister Mary Joseph's Nodule." Dr. Will said, "Of all the splendid surgical assistants I've had, she easily ranks the first."

1893—Edith Graham Mayo, R.N., retired from nursing after marrying Dr. Charlie. She was an integral part of the 98.3 percent success rate in more than 655 surgical operations that were performed at St. Mary's Hospital in its first 4 years.

Alice Magaw, R.N., assumed Edith Graham Mayo's nursing duties and began administering anesthesia with Dr. Charlie. She later published in medical journals and presented at multiple medical societies her success with more than 14,000 patients who were anesthetized without a single death. Dr. Charlie bestowed upon her the title of "The Mother of Anesthesia" for her many achievements.

1906—Saint Marys Hospital Training School for Nurses (later known as Saint Marys Hospital School of Nursing and eventually Saint Marys School of Nursing) was founded by Sister Joseph. Anna Jamme, R.N., visiting Rochester to learn about the hospital, met Sister Joseph after observing her in the operating room. Sister Joseph later appointed Anne Jamme as the school's first superintendent.

1907—In response to pressing demand for more hospital space as well as accommodations for families and friends of patients, Rochester business leader John Kahler opened a facility that combined hospital and hotel services in a renovated house in downtown Rochester. For the next 47 years, the Kahler Corporation continued this model, until it transferred its hospital practice to the not-for-profit Rochester Methodist Hospital.

1910—Dr. Will delivered a commencement speech at Rush Medical College in Chicago that included the phrase, "The best interest of the patient is the only interest to be considered." This statement became the basis of Mayo Clinic's primary value, "The needs of the patient come first."

1916—The Colonial Hotel-Hospital, managed by the Kahler Corporation, opened with nursing school graduates providing patient care. This was significant for patients as nursing school students provided care in most hospitals. The change also was significant for nurses because it opened the way for more graduates to practice in a hospital setting. Until then, professional opportunities for nursing school graduates were largely limited to work as a private duty nurse or a hospital head nurse.

1917-1920—The Stanley, Worrall, and Currie Hospitals opened in downtown Rochester by the Kahler Corporation.

1918—Colonial Hospital Training School for Nurses (forerunner to Kahler School of Nursing and eventually Methodist-Kahler School of Nursing) opened in response to a nursing shortage created when nurses in Rochester and across the country volunteered to serve in World War I.

Florence Bullard, R.N., Saint Marys Hospital Training School Graduate, Class of 1913, was awarded the Croix de Guerre (War Cross) Medal with Bronze Star from the French Government for her heroism during the war. The official citation read: "She has shown imperturbable composure under the most violent bombardments during March and May. Despite her danger, she searched for and comforted and assisted the wounded. Her attitude was especially brilliant on July 31, when bombs burst near."

The worldwide flu epidemic hit Rochester with the first patients admitted to the Isolation Hospital, a converted hotel purchased and remodeled by the Franciscan Sisters to protect the surgical patients from contagious diseases. The epidemic became so severe that 18 nurses were admitted to the hospital for care, one of whom, Sister Agatha O'Brien, R.N., died. Over the next eight months, 360 patients were hospitalized and 41 patients died.

1920S—Nurses and physicians in Rochester began using state-of-the-art treatments including aspirin, digitalis, insulin, x-ray machines, electrocardiographs, suction, and oxygen chambers in caring for patients.

1922—Nursing school curriculum in Rochester included classes in nursing arts, principles and practice of nursing, drugs and solutions, bacteriology, ethics, hospital economics, and bandaging.

Hospital shifts were 6 days a week with 2 hours of rest during the shift if workload permitted.

The Surgical Pavilion (now the Joseph Building) with modern operating rooms, pathology laboratories, and rooms for surgical patients opened at St. Mary's Hospital. Henry Plummer, M.D., commented at the opening about Sister Joseph, "Only

someone of great genius and faith would dare to double the size of this already great hospital...She had the vision and greatness to do it." The pavilion allowed for the rest of St. Mary's and the downtown hospitals to focus on various clinical specialties.

1935—By this time, the nursing school curriculum included classes in fundamentals in nursing, anatomy and physiology, chemistry, pharmacology, first aid, diet in disease, professional problems, medical and surgical nursing, along with specialty classes. In addition to attending classes, student nurses worked 5 to 6 days a week and a half-day on Sundays.

1936—Following the example of the downtown Kahler hospitals, St. Mary's began employing graduate nurses to provide nursing care to patients. Students continued to use the hospital for their clinical experience.

The College of Saint Teresa in Winona began collaborating with St. Mary's Hospital for student clinical experience in its 5-year baccalaureate program. The partnership was mutually beneficial, providing students with a medical-surgical learning experience and providing the hospital with a pool of graduates from which to hire head nurses and nursing instructors.

1937—St. Mary's Hospital admitted its first 2 male nursing students, Emil Zahasky and Telmer Peterson.

1939—Sister Joseph died on March 29. At her funeral, Dr. Will reflected, "As my brother and I look back over the years of her devoted service, we can only say that Sister Mary Joseph has done more for the welfare of the sick than any other woman whom we know. She will be held in honored memory." Dr. Charlie died on May 26 that year, followed by Dr. Will on July 28.

Please note the change to "Saint Marys Hospital." See A Note on Names, page. xv.

1940—With the worldwide polio outbreak beginning to affect Rochester, Sister Elizabeth Kenny from Australia traveled to Rochester, teaching nurses to use hot packs and stretching affected limbs instead of the previous treatment of using splints. As more patients were admitted to Saint Marys Hospital for care and iron lung treatment, Kahler School of Nursing Cadets assisted with care for these patients.

1941—Nurses from Rochester began volunteering to serve in World War II. During the conflict, they were stationed

143

on military bases and hospital ships across the world.

Ruth Erickson, R.N., Kahler School of Nursing Class of 1934, was at the U.S. Naval Hospital in Pearl Harbor, Hawaii, when the Japanese attacked on December 7. She later obtained the rank of captain and was appointed to a 4-year term as director of the United States Navy Corps.

Mayo Clinic sponsored 3 medical units, 2 navy hospitals, and 1 army general hospital to assist with the war effort. Nurses from the Rochester hospitals served in all the units.

1942—Mary Elizabeth Warren, R.N., 1942 graduate of Saint Marys Hospital School of Nursing joined the Army Nurse Corps and received the Silver Star Medal for Valor while in North Africa. Her commendation letter read in part: "Night and day, without thought for yourself, you applied your skill for the saving of lives and the prevention of permanent disability, to the utmost possible, in the battle casualties who came under your care."

1943—The Nurse Training Act (Bolton Act) became law, creating the Cadet Nurse Corps program to help ease the shortage of nurses created by the war. Students who enrolled in the program received nursing school tuition, fees, books, uniforms, and a monthly stipend. Saint Marys Hospital School of Nursing and Kahler School of Nursing trained more than 2,000 cadet nurses to serve their county. In a commitment to diversity and inclusion, the schools admitted and trained more Japanese-Americans women from internment camps as cadets than any other program in the United States.

The Home Nursing Service was started in Rochester, providing free home care to patients after discharge from Saint Marys.

1944—Mary Kiely, R.N., 1930 graduate of Saint Marys Hospital School of Nursing, received the Bronze Star Medal for meritorious service. Her commendation noted that her "professional skill, untiring energy and loyal devotion to duty reflect great credit upon herself and the military services."

The "Mayo Unit," part of the 71st Army General Hospital, organized by Charles W. Mayo, M.D. (Dr. Chuck), and James Priestley, M.D., and staffed almost entirely by Mayo Clinic nurses and physicians, deployed to New Guinea and eventually the Philippines, building hospitals in the jungle and providing care to casualties on both sides of war.

1947—Team nursing began at Saint Marys Hospital with a graduate nurse leading the team and care provided by students, volunteers, and assistants. Each member's skills, knowledge, and judgment were used to provide efficient patient-centered care. The concept was later adopted by the Minnesota League of Nursing Education as way to meet the demand for nursing services.

1948—The Rochester School of Practical Nursing and Homemakers was founded at Saint Marys Hospital. Graduates were able to be licensed as practical nurses and work in key roles in the team nursing model. In 1980, the school changed its name to the Saint Marys School of Practical Nursing.

1950—By this time, the nursing school curriculum included classes in nursing arts, anatomy and physiology, chemistry, microbiology, pharmacology, diet therapy, medical and surgical nursing in addition to more specialty classes such as dermatology and circulatory nursing. A 44-hour work week was allotted for classes and floor experience.

1954—The not-for-profit Rochester Methodist Hospital was established and purchased the Colonial, Worrall, and

Worrall Annex Hospitals and the nursing school from the Kahler Corporation. The nursing school was renamed the Methodist-Kahler School of Nursing.

1955—John Kirklin, M.D., performed the first open-heart surgery on a patient using the heart-lung bypass machine at Rochester Methodist Hospital. Three nurses assisted as part of the surgical team.

1957—After many years of planning and research, the first circular nursing unit, with the nursing station in the center of the unit and patient rooms on the outside, opened at Rochester Methodist Hospital. The design allowed nurses constantly to observe patients directly from the desk, minimizing the amount of walking by staff. In many respects, this model functioned as an early type of intensive care unit.

Saint Marys and Rochester Methodist Hospitals participated in the U.S. Government Foreign Nursing Exchange Program. Nurses from many countries including England, Ireland, Japan, India, and the Philippines worked at the hospitals for 2 years, exchanging best practices, educational methods, and cultural activities with nurses in Rochester. While the formal program ended in 1974, international travel continued to and from Rochester for learning and exchanging of ideas.

1958—The first intensive care units opened at Saint Marys Hospital. The high-tech environment of the intensive care unit (including electrocardiography, oxygen, suction, respirators, and cardiopulmonary resuscitation) called for increased education and professional skills, changing the delivery of nursing care.

1960—The nursing school curriculum was changed to a model of 16 hours in a clinical experience and 8 to 10 hours of class per week. Courses included general education, science, nursing theory, and clinical nursing.

1966—The Summer III program was founded at Rochester Methodist Hospital with 20 junior baccalaureate nursing students in the first group. The program was created to help recruitment and offered students a professional nursing experience in providing direct and indirect nursing care. The program was similar to one that started at Saint Marys Hospital in 1967. The 2 programs were combined in 1991.

1970—The Saint Marys School of Nursing and Methodist-Kahler School of Nursing graduated their last classes after granting more than 7,600 diplomas. The closing of these schools was part of a national trend that moved nursing education from an apprenticeship/practice-based model to the academic environment of colleges and universities. This trend supported the growth of specialized nursing units and the development of professional roles for nurses.

1972—The Nursing Liaison Committee was established between Saint Marys and Rochester Methodist Hospitals. The committee promoted collaboration and program coordination between the hospitals.

Saint Marys and Rochester Methodist Hospitals each established an infection control program with dedicated nurse epidemiologists at each hospital.

A centralized nursing education model began with standardized education by nurse educators with expertise in teaching as their sole responsibility. It replaced the prior model of a unit-based educator and/or unit manager responsible for all orientation and education.

1973—Primary nursing began in one nursing unit at Rochester Methodist Hospital.

In this model, a staff nurse was assigned as the primary nurse to each patient upon admission and had responsibility for the coordination of care throughout the patient's hospital stay. Primary nursing later spread to many inpatient nursing units, eventually evolving into team nursing and then to the current model of relationship-based patient/family-centered care.

1975—The Joint Committee on Nursing Service and Nursing Education began with leaders from both hospitals, local and regional schools of nursing faculty, and public health leaders. The committee focused on facilitating the coordination of nursing clinical facilities and student experiences.

1976—Saint Marys hospital hired its first clinical nurse specialists to serve as practice experts and be available to assist staff nurses with complicated patient care issues. Rochester Methodist Hospital adopted this model in 1981.

Discharge education and planning began as an approach to caring for and giving patients the knowledge and skills to manage their medical conditions at home. As part of the program, a hospital nurse arranged for a public health nurse to follow up when needed.

1978—Rochester Methodist Hospital commissioned a study on the feasibility of a nursing research program. The 2 Ph.D. nurse researchers concluded that "sufficient resources exist within Rochester Methodist Hospital and Mayo Medical Center to support a systemic nursing studies program." The study served as the foundation for the Nursing Research Committee, established in 1989 and the formation of the Nursing Research Division in 1990.

1981—A new patient classification system was implemented, enabling nurses to assess patient care needs to determine the appropriate number of nurses and support staff for the workload from shift to shift.

1982—Nurses began working 12-hour shifts in various intensive care units to promote continuity of patient care.

1983—Rochester Methodist Hospital, in a landmark study by the American Academy of Nursing, was honored as a Magnet Hospital for its ability to attract and retain nurses. The study was the forerunner to the Magnet Recognition Program of today, which recognizes organizations for its quality patient care, nursing excellence, and innovations in nursing practice. Mayo Clinic Hospitals were designated a Magnet facility in 1997 and redesignated in 2002, 2007, and 2011.

1984—Mayo One began helicopter service with staffing by at least one critical care or emergency department flight nurse. Over the next years, Mayo One expanded across southern Minnesota and western Wisconsin with bases in Mankato and Rochester, Minnesota, and Eau Claire, Wisconsin.

1986—Saint Marys Hospital, Rochester Methodist Hospital, and Mayo Clinic formally integrated, establishing a single governing structure to unite services and standardize practice. This milestone event accelerated previous collaboration among nurses from both hospitals and the outpatient practice to integrate nurse recruitment, hiring, staffing, policies and procedures, budgeting, and governance.

1986—Mayo Clinic opened in Jacksonville, Florida, as an adult outpatient specialty care practice with 30 physicians and 120 nurses and allied health staff.

1987—Mayo Clinic opened in Scottsdale, Arizona, as an adult outpatient specialty clinic practice with 42 physicians and 220 nurses and allied health staff.

1989—Mayo Center for Nursing was established to coordinate nursing education, research, and practice across Rochester. In 1993, the Center was incorporated into the Department of Nursing.

1991—Nursing was recognized as a clinical department at Mayo Clinic, aligning nursing as a discipline with other Mayo Clinic departments. Doreen Frusti, R.N., was named Chair, Department of Nursing, and had full accountability and authority for nursing clinical practice.

1992—Mayo Clinic in Rochester began sponsoring national nurse conferences, including a medical and surgical nursing conference, and partnered with Sigma Theta Tau, the honor society of nursing, and Winona State University to hold a nursing research conference. The conferences promoted professional development, the sharing of best practices, and networking.

Mayo Health System, later known as Mayo Clinic Health System, was established as Mayo Clinic began affiliation with regional clinics and hospitals in local communities. Today, the system eventually serves more than 70 communities across 4 states with more than 14,000 nurses and allied health staff.

1994—Saint Marys School of Practical Nursing graduated its last class. The closing of this school reflected a national movement to hire only registered nurses, based on the increasing demands of caring for patients with complex medical needs. Licensed practical nurses were offered the option of remaining in their current positions, transferring to the ambulatory settings, or enrolling in the Department of Nursing educational program to become a registered nurse.

1996—Nurses on inpatient hospital units were offered the choice of colored scrub suits instead of the traditional white uniforms.

1997—Mayo Clinic hired its first certified nurse midwives.

1998—Mayo Clinic Hospital, the first hospital planned, designed, and built by Mayo Clinic, opened in Phoenix, Arizona, with 244 beds and an emergency department.

2003—*Forever Caring,* a bronze tableau of the history of nursing at Mayo Clinic, was dedicated in the Mayo Clinic Nurses Atrium of the Gonda Building. The atrium and the sculpture honor the philanthropic leadership of Marilyn Bateman, R.N., and her husband, Warren.

2003—Mayo Clinic began a 2-year implementation of the electronic medical record in Rochester. This initiative transformed the way nurses and other care providers access, view, record, and communicate medical information.

2005—Nurses in the ambulatory and surgical services integrated into the Department of Nursing, increasing the department's size to 6,200 personnel. Integration of these departments occurred at Mayo Clinic in Florida in 2006, at Mayo Clinic in Arizona in 2012, and at sites across Mayo Clinic Health System, for a total of 13,000 personnel by 2013.

Mayo Clinic benefactors established the joint appointment program with regional schools of nursing. The program enables nurses with graduate degrees to teach while remaining employed at Mayo Clinic.

2006—Nursing at Mayo Clinic in Rochester was awarded the Magnet Prize from the American Nursing Credentialing Center. This prestigious prize recognized Mayo Clinic for its innovation in nursing genomics.

The Mayo Nursing Care Model was developed as the nursing professional practice model at Mayo Clinic in Rochester.

147

The model emphasizes the patient and family as the center of care and recognizes the nurse's relationship in care. The model contains the nursing core values of nurse accountability, professional practice environment, evidence-based practice, and continuity of care. The model also highlights the role of the nurse in the dimensions of vigilant guardian, problem solver, transformational leader, caring healer, pivotal communicator, teacher, and navigator.

2007—The Nursing Leadership Perspectives Program began for staff registered nurses. The program promotes professional nursing and increases awareness of shared governance, interdisciplinary collaboration and leadership skills.

2008—Mayo Clinic in Rochester was named a Best Workplace for Men in Nursing by the American Assembly for Men in Nursing. This designation recognized Mayo's leadership in recruiting and retaining men and having a workplace culture that supports men in nursing.

Mayo Clinic opened a hospital on the Jacksonville, Florida, campus attached to the outpatient practice. At its opening, the hospital had 214 beds and an emergency department.

The Mayo Clinic Enterprise Nursing Committee structure, with representatives from Rochester, Florida, Arizona, and Mayo Clinic Health System, was established. Under this umbrella, multiple committees focus on clinical practice, education, evidence-based practice, informatics, and quality. These efforts helped lead to a single standardized nursing practice across all Mayo locations.

2010—Nurse-to-nurse bedside handoffs began in Rochester with diffusion to all sites. The practice focuses on involving patients in their care and standardizing communication between nurses at shift change.

Doreen Frusti, R.N., was named the first Chief Nursing Officer of Mayo Clinic, providing leadership, guidance, and direction on nursing practice to all Mayo Clinic sites.

2011—Pamela Johnson, R.N., was named Chief Nursing Officer of Mayo Clinic and chair of the Department of Nursing in Rochester.

2013—Mayo Clinic named Jason Fratzke, R.N., as Chief Nursing Informatics Officer. In this role, he is responsible for strategic and operational leadership in the development, deployment, and integration of clinical information systems to support nurses and allied health staff in patient care.

2014—Mayo Clinic recognized 150 years of continuous service to patients, with nursing as an integral part of the Mayo Clinic Model of Care.

Index

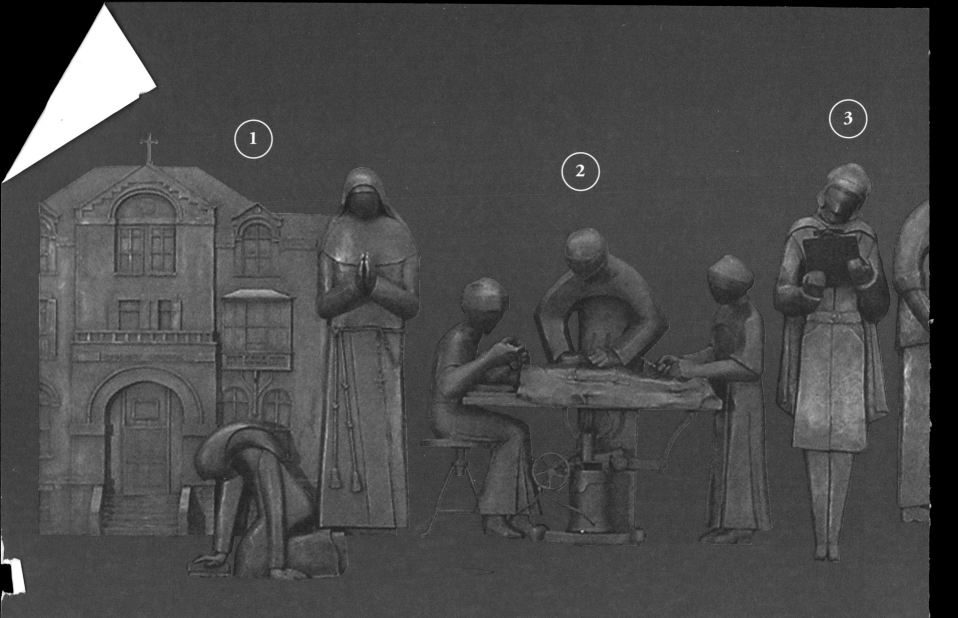

Forever Caring

Created by Gloria Tew and named by Bridget Dean, this bronze tableau is displayed in the Mayo Nurses Atrium of the Gonda Building at Mayo Clinic in Rochester, Minnesota. It was commissioned to honor the history of nursing at Mayo Clinic and to recognize the philanthropic leadership of Marilyn Bateman, R.N., and her husband, Warren.

Forever Caring depicts the evolution of nursing at Saint Marys Hospital and the Kahler hospitals/Rochester Methodist Hospital, along with their respective schools of nursing. The tableau also represents key contributions of nursing to the three primary activities of Mayo Clinic—patient care, research, and education. These activities are represented as three interlocking shields in the logo of Mayo Clinic.

Spiritual and human values are shown in nurses throughout the tableau. Representing diverse traditions and areas of specialization, they speak to the ongoing dedication of nurses in all locations to help fulfill the mission of Mayo Clinic.

1. This figure represents the history of nursing at Saint Marys Hospital, founded in 1889 by the Sisters of Saint Francis.
2. The nurse anesthetist (left) is engaged in patient care.
3. The nurse, wearing a Saint Marys School of Nursing cap, is engaged in research.
4. Contemporary figures of a female and male nurse show the response of the nursing profession to current and future patient care needs.
5. A nurse, wearing the Methodist-Kahler School of Nursing cap, cares for a patient in a wheelchair.
6. The graduate nurse is involved with education.
7. A nurse holds an infant, representing care as the essence of nursing.
8. A nurse, holding a patient tray, wears a cap from Saint Marys School of Practical Nursing.
9. This figure represents the history of nursing in downtown Rochester, Minnesota. The Kahler hospital system was founded in 1907. Rochester Methodist Hospital, which assumed its role in providing inpatient care, was established in 1954.